# OF FEAR

# AND

# FREEDOM

# OF FEAR
# AND
# FREEDOM

## CARLO LEVI

*Author of* CHRIST STOPPED AT EBOLI

*Translated from the Italian by Adolphe Gourevitch*

*New York · 1950*
*Farrar, Straus and Company*

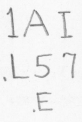

# CONTENTS

| | |
|---|---|
| Translator's Preface | vii |
| Author's Preface | xiii |
| I. Ab Jove Principium | 1 |
| II. Sacrifice | 13 |
| III. Love Sacred and Profane | 25 |
| IV. Slavery | 41 |
| V. The Muses | 58 |
| VI. Blood | 78 |
| VII. Mass | 107 |
| VIII. Sacred History | 124 |

# TRANSLATOR'S PREFACE

It is not usual for a translator to speak in his own name. But this is a rather unusual book, and the job of preparing a version for the American reader has been quite an adventure in itself—which may or may not justify a few words of explanation (about the Italian original) and of apology (about the "translation").

Carlo Levi's *Paura della libertà—Fear of Freedom,* or rather: *Of Fear and Freedom*—is a short book, almost a booklet, which does not solve but does clearly state the biggest problem in the world, the most important question, fact or figure man has ever had to consider: namely, himself. The subject of this shrewd historical analysis, or study of social psychology, the hero of this epic poem and sacred drama, is nothing or nobody in particular, everything, everybody in general: our father Adam, you and I, your folks and mine, the collective and individual monster.

Monster: as every word in this author's language, one must take it at its face value, remembering that a value, not unlike Janus, has always more than one face. Man is still the greatest beast in Paradise, the marvel of creation wherever he looks. And whenever he looks at himself, at his own world, upon the surface of all the waters and deep into every sky, he shrinks away from his own image, and replaces it by another image of his own, by another *idol*; by the ambiguousness of his gracious and fearful gods, the gods of ambiguity.

And here comes Carlo Levi, going into the very depth of the mirror without making faces. He describes what he sees—which is a work of wisdom. And he pictures it as he sees it, which is a work of beauty. For Carlo Levi is a physician and a painter, a writer and and fighter for liberty—that is true. But mainly he is a genius: like the child in Andersen's tale, he can tell a king by his nakedness, and draw a masterpiece out of it.

To what literary genre does this book belong?

Classifying would be idleness. *Of Fear and Freedom*—in our humble judgment—pertains to science as well as to poetry: which in all of Adam's days were not, or should not have been divided.

It would be even less useful to define the author's philosophy, or political opinions, or general credo. The critics' guesses—if any—might be as good or bad as our own comments. The true reader shall read this little book time and again (at least as far as the original is concerned) and may be trusted to find the answers by himself. However, the vast majority of those who will not read it at all, or peruse it only once, might feel too certain about the writer's views and conclusions. And therefore, perhaps, a warning is not quite superfluous.

Although Carlo Levi describes the history, society and psychology of man from the starting point of religion, he is by no means a religious philosopher, nor a mere sociologist of religion, nor a believer in any definite deity. And while he exposes each and every idol, Carlo Levi should not be mistaken for an iconoclast, as he shows the inevitable, the legitimate function of idolatry in every religion—be it a church or a state, or the most private, personal faith and intimate conviction.

This book contains a lucid, fearless, ruthless, sometimes impudent criticism—an unanswerable criticism—of everything man adores: himself and his woman, his individual and collective self, the mass and the race, the class and the state, their freedom and slavery, their peace and their wars. This is a light which illuminates the dark foundations, but does not burn down the great temple of Adam. A remorseless, poetical light, revealing at one stroke the eternal outlines. A vision through every sacred dogma of virtue and love, of social utopism and national pride. A vivisection of clannishness and feudalism, monarchy and revolution, of all the fascisms and all the liberations.

But nowhere does the author give preference to his own ideals or idols of liberty. He does not preach and propagate a doctrine of his own, nor plead for any particular form of salvation, nor state peremptorily any universal truth. Except maybe the one which "manifests *itself* before the open eyes": a truth too naked for the taste of our generation, or of any generation since the great fall.

For ". . . night's darkness dwells in the depth of man: upon the works of man the sun is shining."

Every translation is a betrayal. Especially in the

case of a booklet of such magnitude. Therefore, our first reaction, when asked by our friend Carlo Levi to put the thing into English without betraying it, was —after careful reading and pondering—to refuse energetically. But once the poison is in the blood, there is no other cure but to pass it on; and so we undertook the task, with passion and almost with despair, struggling through a few sentences a day, and playing with the golden words of Italy—in the hope of conveying to the American reader some faint image of this gem of beauty, some idea about this wise poem of timeless truth.

It has been worked in the style of the Mediterra-nean, a style of which Carlo Levi is a peculiar master, and in which the delicate and intricate precision of Latin expression blends with the ancient powers of the Hebrew word. A sensuous and musical sorcery of logic and magic at once.

There was no hope of translating it into real American, into the vernacular of the states—whose great qualities and particular limitations differ entirely from those required; a language, anyhow, into which a writer must be born, for no stranger can possibly *learn* it. So the only way open was to make use of a historical peculiarity which distinguishes literary

English: its ability to swallow up an extraordinary amount of Latin forms and words without losing its own identity and without becoming utterly incomprehensible.

We do not claim, therefore, to have *translated* this Latin song of Adam, but only to have rephrased it to the point where any cultured American (who does not know the Italian language) may listen to it without undue effort, and feel its rhythm and melody, both philosophical and verbal, and gain at least an inkling of what he has lost by not being able to hear the original Italian.

A. G.

# AUTHOR'S
# PREFACE

I wrote this book in a time which seems already remote, not so much because of the seven years that
have passed, but because of the many events that took
place within in this short period. To those men who
in some peculiar and often miraculous manner have
survived, these events, whether unexpected or not,
brought an experience of suffering, of blood and of
death such as cannot be measured by the common
yardstick of time. And today, that which was happening prior to this interlude of slaughter seems gone
forever, even if perchance our thoughts have not
changed, or we have taken again to our old habits,
and found once more the ways of long ago.

It was then that the crisis which was beclouding

the life of Europe for several decades, and which had manifested itself in all the rifts, problems, difficulties, cruelties, heroism and tedium of our time, resolved itself into a catastrophe.

War had begun, the German armored divisions were overrunning the plains of Poland. From my house on the shore of the Atlantic I could watch daily the incoming English troopships, which were disembarking the first British army in the harbor of Saint Nazaire.

The French soldiers were leaving, in their shabby uniforms with the fustian trousers, wearing the annoyed faces of pacifists vowed to defeat; the English were arriving, a sixteenth-century army from a revived *Merry England,* drunken and impudent, amateur warriors who were the terror of the Catholic women of Brittany, and cheerfully sure of a victory, no matter how remote.

Traditional military values seemed entirely upset: but not only military values. All the data of a civilization were dissolving in mist; an uncertain future was lying in wait, uncertain for the world, and for each single individual. The old ideologies, all of them, were apparently collapsing, exhausted by sterile criticism and by futile defense: a wind of death and of obscure religion was shaking the ancient states of Europe.

On the beach of La Baule the wind was blowing and lifting with a slight rustle the white subtle shells, tenuous skeletons of the dead leaves of the sea. The past was fading away as into another life, beyond the chasm of war. Normal life, the continuity of generations and institutions, was at an end. The new gods of the state were blowing away from the world human values and even the sense of time. To protect themselves men had to accept this barrenness of slaughter, to abandon their houses and families, to discard at one stroke everything they had lived for, and even the memory of childhood's ties.

It was then that I was informed of the unexpected death of my father: the closed borders had prevented me from seeing him before the end. At this point of life where there was no turning back, I found myself alone on a deserted beach, in a bleak autumn, full of wind and rain.

The past being dead, the present uncertain and frightful, the future dark with mystery, one felt the need to look around and take one's bearings; to stop and consider the reasons for the bloody revolution which was taking shape.

Thus I resolved to write (for myself alone and without any thought of publication, for at that time such a thought would have been quite absurd) a book which according to its first outline should have been rather lengthy: after a general description of the contemporary crisis in its entirety (for I had no doubts about the strict interdependency of its various aspects), there was to be a series of analyses, taking up each problem separately. In other words, the book would have consisted of an introduction, showing the common deep causes of the crisis, and seeking them not so much in this or that particular event, but rather in the very soul of man; and of many chapters dealing with each single subject from politics (with a critical analysis of ideologies, both liberal and socialistic) and art (including a history of modern art) to science, philosophy, religion, technical progress, social life, customs, etc.

I began to write under the conditions described, with the poetic pleasure of discovery. I had no books at my disposal, and no documentation pertaining to any of the particular problems. After I had written the first eight chapters I was forced to interrupt my work and return to Paris. In the following months I had no time to write; then there followed the defeat of the French and the flight before Hitler's armies. The Germans entered Paris, the German flag was hoisted upon the Tour Eiffel, on that fourteenth of June which may well remain as a symbolic date marking the end of a world of civilization, of art, of culture, a world that will never come back, even if today it does not seem to have been replaced by anything else of a definite character.

I was not able to continue the book because of these external obstacles; but also, and chiefly, because I noticed that such as it was, my book—for me —was finished. What I had written was approximately the introduction or preface to the work outlined above, but all the particular developments which I had had in mind were implicit therein. I had tried to reach the core of the world I was describing, to immerse myself into that ambiguous hell: because of this writing *from the inside,* the style of the book had assumed a poetic and religious character which arose directly from its subject. Considering this effort to achieve identification and unity (in addition to the practical reasons, obvious to anybody who was writing at that time in European countries subject to tyranny, where the art of allusion had become the most important of all literary expedients), I felt that the book already contained everything I intended to state, and that it ought not be developed in a more explicit way. There was in it a theory of Nazism, although Nazism is not mentioned even once by name; there was a theory of the state and of liberty; there was a theory of esthetics, of religion, of sin, etc. The book remained as it was, without addition. I brought it, secretly, to Italy in 1941; and many friends advised me to publish it at once. But, of course, no Italian publisher could at that time take the risk of these too obvious symbols.

Recently, after seven years, and after all that has happened, I had to decide whether it was still worth while to publish it, and if so, whether I ought to postpone the publication, to transpose the book into expository language, into political and historical terms, and to reveal the symbols (already quite transparent) by adding to them all the results of accumulated experience. But, quite apart from the fact that such a work of improvement and transposition would be very difficult for me, or even impossible, it seemed to me that it was preferable not to change the manuscript at all, so that it should retain the character of a document about a time in which we have lived with such intensity. The book—as I have said—

was written for myself alone, without any thought of publication: therefore it has the character, which is that of a "confession." Certain lands thus discovered are not visited twice; and there is a world of present activities which prevents us from plunging again into that lake of barbarism, from re-entering that forest, those Middle Ages of the soul. Therefore I have refrained from changing even one word in the original draft, and from correcting even those parts which seem to me the weakest and the least ready for immediate publication. It appeared to me that this little book (so different from my *Christ Stopped at Eboli,* which was written five years later) should be allowed to keep its own time element, for in this time element, perhaps, resides its value of expression. If I am wrong, I beg the reader to forgive me.

C. L.

*Rome, January 1946*

# I.

# AB JOVE
# PRINCIPIUM

*Ab Jove principium*—everything begins with Jupiter. And we too must begin there, at this non-existent point from which all things are born. Our Jupiter, however, we need not seek in the skies, but where he is wont to stay, in places most dark and earthly, in the maternal dampness of the deep. He is more akin to the worm than to the eagle; but soon enough, he will find his own heraldic eagles, and extol them above every badge or emblem, for only thus will he avoid being devoured, once and for all, by the true eagles of the heavens.

Beyond metaphors, we cannot grasp anything human, unless we start from the feel of *the sacred*: the most ambiguous, deep-seated, double-edged of all feelings and senses, worm and eagle alike; a con-

1

tinuous dark denial of freedom and art, and—conversely—a continuous creation of art and freedom.
And again, we cannot understand anything social,
unless we start from the meanings of *religion*, this
disrespectful heir of things sacred.

What is the process of every religion? To change
the *sacred* into the *sacrificial*: to deprive it of its
main feature—inexpressibility—by transforming it
into deeds and words; to create the ritual out of the
mythical; to substitute a sacramental bird for a
shapeless turgidity, and marriage for desire; to turn
sacred suicide into consecrated slaughter. Religion
is relation and relegation. Relegation of a god into
a web of formulas, conjurations, invocations, prayers, so that he may not, as is his way, elude us.
Sacredness, the very appearance of terror, shapes itself into law, in order to escape its own self. Pure
anarchy becomes pure tyranny. Man, as a free being,
is thus bound by the selfsame bonds of the sacred,
and relegated into a common reciprocal nexus before the deity. There is no rabble without a king,
there are no masses without God. It may be false to
claim that every society grows out of a religious tie;
but it is certainly true that every monarchy is reli-

2

gious. Every king, great or small, every petty prince and clan chieftain is a sacred majesty: a being divinely ambiguous, having no true name, except a name symbolic and heraldic (a number); a being that lives hidden or perhaps may not live at all; a being the less existent the more it appears to be. With good reason the most ancient kings—true kings—were beasts or indeterminate powers of nature; and thus China was ruled by dragon-kings, by tiger-kings, by demon-kings,—and Egypt, by dog-faced and falcon-headed royal gods.

The nearer the formless sense of sacredness swims up to the surface of men's consciousness, the less certain, the more earthly and manifold are the religious shapes into which it flows and ends. The deeper the sacred sinks into our inner recesses, the higher the gods soar into the cloudless sky; and when the sacred in ourselves is reduced to a disappearing center, to a single point, fiery but extremely remote—then the One God hides beyond the clouds, out of time, out of space, shrouded in total transcendence. But when even this vanishing point is forgotten, and the mass grows into person, God himself loses existence, while the blue skies of day and the black skies of night

3

cease to watch us like open eyes and change into fields of serene contemplation, or into wastes tempestuously human, aerial mirrors of the soul.

So, too, the kings and the idols. In times of sacred lore they must be monsters, stones and trees, and ambiguous terrors of darkness; in times when religion prevails, they are shepherds, patricians, animals, and thereafter monarchs and images—until the day when a red Phrygian cap on the head of a Louis crowns constitutional kings, dead kings, worshipped guillotines. But in the short interludes of liberty the kings are forgotten, the idols entombed. These interludes, like the others (needless to say), do not form an historical progression: they are subjective, they coexist. Everybody is born from chaos, and to chaos may revert; every man leaves the mass in a process of differentiation, and in this shapeless mass may lose himself again. But the only vivid moments in an individual life, the only periods of higher culture in history are those in which the two contrary processes of differentiation and undifferentiation find a common point of equilibrium and are coexistent in the creative act.

What is undifferentiation and how is it related to sacredness? The myth of creation out of chaos is

4

truly full of sense. There is a primeval indistinctness, common to all men, flowing in eternity, inherent to every aspect of the world, spirit of every being in the world, memory of all time of the world. All individuals start from it, urged by an obscure freedom to break loose and gain their own individual forms, and perpetually drawn back by an obscure necessity and compelled to merge again in this same indistinction. This twofold endeavor stretches from one death to another: from prenatal chaos to the natural fading away and extinction. But only a total detachment from this everlasting indefinite flow, only a void and egoistic reasoning, only the abstraction of liberty are really and truly death—as are their opposites: complete lack of self-differentiation, mystic brutish darkness, the bondage of the inexpressible.

The flow of indistinction is *nature* itself, obscure beyond utterance, whose sighs are earthquakes and volcanoes, storms and constellations—and the unerring unconsciousness of the insect. *Action,* on the contrary, is the outcome of complete differentiation: the individual, severed from the whole, moves on to find his own shape, and his motion has a meaning only to himself. And again, action must be distinguished from *achievement,* which results from creative human activity, and blends at the very same moment individual riches and the treasures of universality—differentiation and undifferentiation: an activity most individual when soaring above the individuals, and most universal when intensely singular; born of freedom and necessity at once; understood by all men through man's common indistinct nature; transcending everyone, inasmuch as every man is a distinct, single self; but shared by everyone in the free process of individuation and consciousness.

The feeling of a transcendent indistinctness and the terror of it, the dread of indetermination which dwells in those who are in the very act of giving birth to themselves, of severing themselves from the mass—this is the *sacred*.

The way of *religion* is to substitute that which is undifferentiated and inexpressible with concrete images and symbols—so that the sacred may be cast out of our consciousness and replaced by finite, and therefore liberating, objects. That which is common to man and wolf is, through sheer indistinction, a boundless terror—until a totemic image turns it into bearable worship. That which is common to man and

6

man is a mysterious original sin never committed, the transgression of a limit, of all limits, and the agony of the unlimited; until a god man comes to free us, by substituting himself for sin, by burdening himself with sin.

Religion is therefore, thus considered, a means in the process of individuation; but a means which, in order to liberate the spirit from the terrifying feeling of transcendency, tends to replace it by visible symbols, by *idols*.

Man does not stand alone before the sky and before his own self. Facing the "I" there is the *other*—all the others, mankind. Every human relation, before it becomes free, must be sacred and religious—for relationship is possible only through the "I" being also the "other," to the point of identity. Closed in himself, the individual tends to separate and live an autonomous life: contact with others is allowed only through that which is common to all, only through the undifferentiated, whose perennial presence renders comprehensible every differentiation. Truly human intercourse, therefore, is always a return to the origins, and that is where shyness and bashfulness arise. The fear of the woman is a sacred horror, for

in the act of love every personal memory is blurred
—drowned in the universal indistinct memory of the
waters of Chaos.

Each truly human relationship breeds, thus, the
sense of sacredness, every temporary liberation must
be religious in character, must mean the substitution
of man by his own symbol, by the idol of his own
person. Such is the origin of personal names, family
names, coats of arms and banners. A man not free
enough to establish communications with his fellows
without getting lost, will choose, instead of the actual
human intercourse, a purely symbolic relationship,
enabling him to remain within himself; and even of
his own self each man makes an idol, for fear of
reaching, through intimate exploration, those mysterious depths where each self melts away.

That which holds true of the intercourse between
individual men, applies equally to the relations of
man, society and the state: not only because they, too,
are human relationships, but also because society and
the state, to those men who do not perceive them as
embodiments of their own freedom, must appear as
towering giants above understanding. The farther
the state is removed from each individual, the might-
ier it grows in boundless leviathanic complexity, the

more it breeds an all-pervasive sense of sacredness. And to relieve us from this sacred horror, society and the state must change into gods.

In the first social nucleus, in the primitive state of the clan, the father is the god. His deification suppresses every truly human intercourse with his kinsmen. He stays in his tent, his appearances are unfrequent; he has the power of blessing and cursing, and his is the right to kill—a right of heroes, not of men. Every attempt to enter into closer relationship with the father appears both anarchical and atheistic, and incest is therefore abominable. Incest deprives Lot of his divine authority, for—his ways being entirely those of nature—he cannot, like Jupiter, change into a bull, a cloud, a golden rain for his miraculous embraces of women. The greatest political offence is that of Ham, son of Noah, who discovers his father's nakedness, because he wants to see his father as a human being. Ambiguity—the transition from the real father to the image of the father-god, and the feeling of profanation in seeing the former through the latter—this is the chief origin of the father-complexes. (As for the mother-complexes —whose mechanism is sometimes the same—conditions seem to be entirely reversed: mother and son

9

continue almost physically to be one and the same; the attempted severance and glorification do not succeed, and the complex results from this failure).

The deification of the father (and the complexes that ensue) last as long as the son's infancy, until the son, peering into himself, perceives himself equal to the father, entirely a man. The deification of the state (and the resulting servitude) will last as long as social infancy, until each man examines his own self and finds in his own complexity the entire structure of the state, and in his own freedom—the necessity of the state. The act of Noah's son is therefore a real sacrilege and political offence—Ham being still in his infancy and not yet seeking in his self the father and the state, but viewing them as gods and himself as son and slave: a rebellious son and slave, not a man free from bondage.

Thus, the state-idol marks at once the need of true human relations and the incapacity to establish them freely; it denotes both the sacred nature of these relations and the inability to differentiate them without drying them up; and above all, it is the sign of man's dread of man. This terror of self forms the deepest-rooted of all idolatries, for its fount is ever present, and the most monstrous of all, for it is entirely human. But this idolatry presupposes the sense of an absolute identity of men, and the fear of not being distinguished as *persons*: the sense of a *mass*, of a shapeless humanity, where every individual limit is arbitrary, because the individuals are not really defined. Its opposite is to be found in abstract individualism, wherein every sense of community is lost, while the state, far from being deified, does not even exist, because *passions* are non-existent. This atheism is no less deadly than the idolatry mentioned above. It is useless to be free *from* passions: we ought to be free *in* our passions. For passion is the place where each individual meets the undifferentiated universe; it is the fecundity of sleep everlasting, the eternal return to earlier indistinction—and the problem is to remain ourselves, to retain freedom, in this necessary return.

Abstract individualism, flight from passion, inability to sleep, are nothing but barrenness. But dread of passion, fear of sleeping, the feel of the darkness we are made of, the horror of night's shadow without light—this is the black religion of the state. And, as no Faustian deed is either dream or passion—so, too, none of the thousand cries calling a people to "wake up" can free them from the weight of their slumber, and from the monsters they adore. Only the process of inner maturation will turn the totemic beast, the intangible father, the sacred majesty into the lovely adornments of the past; and then, the temples of Mars, of Vesta, of Janus, and the ceremonial antiquities of England, will remind adult nations that they, too, were infants in days of yore. Good care will be taken, then, of the memories and the myths, which will survive in customs and figures of speech—but so remote as to become incomprehensible. Every word we speak is saturated with religions past and spent; A flight of birds stirs us, because in a faraway time (faraway, though not bygone) it used to be an omen.

This is true on a personal level as well as on the level of history: that which has been may return once more, that which has been hidden deep may crop out on the surface of our consciousness—like the sands which appear again with the turn of the tide.

# II.

# SACRIFICE

Religion's peculiar process, as we have said, is to change the sacred into the sacrificial, to transform suicide into consecrated slaughter, and anarchy into tyranny. There is no religion without sacrifice: the two terms may be considered altogether equivalent, (even though sacrifice is only a part, an insuppressible modality of religion), for sacrifice denotes a sacred act as well as the killing of the sacred. This primordial necessity, present at every initial phase of religion, cannot be understood when judged by the standards of practical, juridical, contractual reasoning. Tame religions, remote from their origins, no longer sacrifice; they make offerings. Only those who are free from a god can turn to him as to an equal, asking for his gifts and giving to him in exchange. In Lucania, during the procession of the rustic, black-faced Madonna, people throw grain upon her, thus reminding an avaricious earth to grant us another harvest—and also as a due tribute, like those gifts of wheat, animals and eggs, which are brought to the lord of the place whenever one enters his mansion. An infinite number of candles are being lit all over the world, before the images of the saints, that they may bear in mind our needs, and by the flaming lights keep memory of our souls. If formerly such acts were sacrifices, by now they have lost their ancient significance, retaining only its shadow and becoming mere human gestures of gratitude, repayment and good omen, even though they are aimed not at humans, but at the likeness of gods. Even the usual meaning of the word sacrifice, denoting voluntary loss, renouncement, detachment, differs in part from its original meaning. Sacrifice is a detachment, a severance, but a bloody severance; it is an act of death, accomplished in order to gain life: it is a religious operation. In the place of sacred indistinction, religion offers us a name and a divine shape, which prevent us from losing ourselves in sacredness, which keep us from suicide and anarchy, which grant us the privilege of living. But this repellent sacredness exerts

14

nevertheless an irresistible attraction; the divine and adored shape, by the very act of adoration, loses its outlines and efficacy and fades into that indistinction from which it originated. In order that the god may live, severance from the sacred must actually take place; the god himself must be not only created and worshipped, but hated and killed. Only the sacramental slaying of the god allows the god to exist: the less he merges with ourselves, but stays aloof and strange and foreign, the greater is his reality. And to make him such, there is no other means than to kill him according to a rite. That is why, whenever a god appears in human guise, it is always in the guise of a stranger, an alien traveler, someone out of another world. Therefore, strangers are gods for those people to whom they reveal themselves for the first time. And therefore, the guest is sacred and cannot be asked his name; while the enemy, the foreigner, is sacred too, but in the opposite sense, and must be killed. *Hostis* and *hostia* are one and the same. Everything is ambiguous in such acts, for that relation with sacredness which brings them forth is ambiguity itself. Here love and hatred, communion and death, do truly coincide, or give birth to one another. In order not to melt away in mystic fusion with the sacred, in order not

15

to die in God, there must be either the freedom of a completed person, or else another death, the death of the god himself, or of the object deified. None of these two ends may stand without the other: without previous suicide, this death has no efficacy and shrinks to an empty ritual act. Idols are the offspring of a fearful attraction: conversely, an idol can be real only through the relationship of an adoring estrangement. Separation, denial and killing—these are truly the acts which breed the reality of a god. Liberating symbol of an elusive, illimitable reality, the deity has a power of its own inasmuch as it is limited and limitable, and can be denied. The sacrifice of the god (or of a substitute) is at once the affirmation of his existence and the testimony of his reality. The world of rites estranges the incumbent sacredness, and, conversely, turns sacred everything alien and strange. Every alienation is idol-worship, and there is no idolatry without alienation. In this sense, the victim is always the god, and the god always the victim. Therefore, the agony of the most obscure and tremendous human sin, perhaps the only human sin, the sin of origin, the severance from the formless, the fall into separation, could be redeemed, in the realm of religion, only by the ritual killing of the truest of gods, of the most human of men, of the only one to whom nothing was alien and nothing sacred, for in him, the divine and the human coexisting, there was no original sin.

Thus, the process of sacrifice and that of religion are one and the same—they are both acts of aliena·tion. Therefore, the victim must share the nature of the idol, thus enabling the idol to become estranged and to draw life from this estrangement; or else, the victim must be of the opposite nature, of a nature alien to the idol, and for this very reason conse-crated. But always remaining the image of an awe-inspiring communion and the point where each in-dividual loses his limit, the idol—be it a stone or a tree, an animal or a monster, a father, a king or a god—always completely unites with the individual adorer; and therefore, the true sacrifice, the true act of denial of this unity, shall be the alienation of man himself, or of a part of him. Hence the common meaning of the word sacrifice as renouncement, even outside its religious acceptation; and of course there is no religion without renouncement. Something of the sacrificer, a thing which is the sacrificer, some-thing of the idol and which is the idol, has to be voluntarily estranged and destroyed. Only such religious mutilation allows men to live. A mutilation which may consist of a mere obstacle or restriction, or of the loss of a human function or activity, leading even to the point of detachment from earthly goods, of seclusion in the desert. To gods of fecundity and generation are dedicated sacred virgins, or on the contrary—orgiastic mysteries: opposite sacrifices, but of an identical nature. This is the magic origin of vows, of interdictions, of prohibitions which ban certain acts, certain foods, and forbid sexual contacts with women made sacred by pregnancy or by recent delivery. And this is why certain parts of the body become sacred, unmentionable, shameful, and have to be hidden. Something of man must of necessity become strange to man, for the sake of a new life which starts and develops in accordance with religious initiation; something of man must be renounced, expelled, chased out, cut off, to make this life possible. Such is one of the meanings of circumcision, this concrete and localized anticipation of the crucifixion.

So that the god may live, man—in every idolatry —must become estranged from his own self, and victim unto himself: for the god is not God, and man is not yet man. To the deities of nature, bred by the

18

terror of woods, by the mystery of harvests, by physical communion with animals, belong the sacrifice of bullocks and kids, of fruits and crops and firstlings. To the fires of heaven respond the votive fires of forests, and the birth-giving floods are matched by immersions in water, by lustral washings—innocuous symbols of mortal surrenders. But wherever human fright has engendered an idol, the victim shall be human: if not actually a human, at least a symbol of man. Where we have a tribe, and the tribesman is uncertain whether to leave animality or enter it again, sacred animals and men are slain together before beastlike and ambiguous idols: the werewolf issues forth by night in search of victims, and cannibalism is religion. Immortal Minotaurs are nourished forever, in labyrinths and outside labyrinths, upon the flesh of Athenian maidens. Giants and monsters and sphinxes are always awaiting a Theseus, an Hercules, an Oedipus, these liberators from physical uncertainty, these destroyers of double-faced idols and founders of religions preponderantly human. Every wood, every lake, every piece of land holds its feudal dragon, which preys upon men, maids and peasants; and the knight-errant who slays them only substitutes one dynasty for another. Paternal deities, like Saturn, devour their children, and children consummate to all eternity, in their wishes and their actions, the sacrifice of the father. The kings, having put off the vesture of dragons, continue to feed in a religious sense upon their subjects; regicide, in its turn, consecrates the kings.

Every primitive clan, ruled by deified patriarchs, and consequently every patrician state, rests upon sacrifice. In these states, the stranger is sacred; *adversus hostem aeterna auctoritas esto*.* But the son himself must be made a stranger: Esau is dispossessed, Ishmael chased away, both necessary victims, and there dies Iphigenia. The first born must be immolated; and they are immolated, as long as the law of the heroes endures; they are carried by their godlike fathers to the high places where blood must flow. And this occurs until Abram bows to a greater and remoter god, and becomes Abraham, a mere human father, divested of any divine attribute, a priest to the universal deity. Then, naturally, the knife falls from his hand, and a ram is substituted for the first-born son: because the new god is no longer the deity of a clan, of a tribe, or of the *patres*, but a true God. Furthermore, such a God being ab-

* Law of the XII Tables.

20

solutely transcendent and having nothing in common
with man, human sacrifice becomes utterly impossible: there remain only crude memories of a former
religion of blood, the lamb and circumcision, which
is symbolic (this is its secondary meaning) of the
slaughter of the first born.

In each of its more complex forms, whenever it is
not built upon freedom or made subservient to other
ideals, but is considered as a deity in itself, as an
idol requiring adoration, the state—like the divi-
nised clan, or tribe, or patriciate—can live only on
human sacrifice. Although the ancient prisoner,
crowned with flowers or bound in chains, is slain no
more upon the altar, the religion of the state requires,
in sacrificial form, the renouncement, surrender and
death of something human. Without self-mutilation
man cannot make a god out of his own capacity for
human relations, that is—out of his ability to shape
the state; nor can he free himself religiously from the
dread of these relations, from the anxiety of belonging to an indistinct mass. On the individual level, the
necessary sacrifice is to renounce autonomy, to accept
an infinite series of interdictions and observances, to
perceive as justly inaccessible the functions of the
state, and to sense as irreverent any desire of grasp-

ing them, of sharing in any way the so-called "exercise of sovereignty." The *secret of state* truly becomes the secret of a temple: the layman dare not approach it. If man's power of ruling himself is to be turned into an idol, the very manhood of man must be ceaselessly rejected and expelled as a thing sacred, unmentionable, disgraceful.

On the social level, the necessary sacrifice must be the mutilation of a part of society. A group, a class, a nation must be forcibly driven out, treated as enemies, turned into strangers, so that they may become the god's witnesses and victims. And conversely, the strangers are sacred and must die, while warriors become sacrificers, to be sacrificed in their turn.

Without the awareness of this dark necessity, which makes every god true, every servitude willing, every victim sacred; which indissolubly binds the lord and the slave, the king and the prisoner, the banner and exile; without this sense of religious limitation which drives the world on its adored and blood-stained ways, history would be incomprehensible. Joseph de Maistre, to prove the providential nature of war, uses for arguments the impossibility of explaining it by human motives, its lack of proportion, its futility and unreasonableness. Tested by a purely rationalistic examination, not war alone appears impossible, but slavery as well, and privilege, and wealth, and kingship itself, and almost every historical institution. History becomes meaningless, or an arcane mystery,

> . . . which Fate impels by dark enchantment upon its ways,*

or a chaotic mix-up, where the sorcerer may search, if he will, for magic relations of numbers and events; or an absurd adventure of an eternal deceit by priests and tyrants, to which only the light of reason can put an end, by starting a new age of fully explained truth. In truth, the light of reason cannot illuminate this darkness, but only burn these idols and turn them into barren cinders. Beneath this purificatory aridity, darkness will continue to dwell in us, more fathomless and sombre than before. At the beginning of time—so we are told—there was a forest upon the face of the earth. This same primeval forest—shapeless and full of seeds and terrors, hiding in its

---

* *Lo spinge il Fato con oscuro incanto*
  *per le sue vie . . .*
  (Tommaso Campanella—*Poesie*)

blackness the features of every face—we bear in ourselves; from it began our earthly journey; and again we find it in the middle of the way, with all its fear; youthful woodland of unlimited powers. Outside liberty, outside creative freedom, every activity, every definition of this infinite potency is but a limitation, a distress, an endless pain, and a sense of irretrievable loss—because every religion is sacrifice and surrender. The first men, according to myth, wandered through boundless woods until they stopped in *certain* places, loved *certain* women and worshipped *certain* gods. And even now, man wanders through an eternal forest, in search of an external certainty: a certainty whose price is servitude and death.

# III.

# LOVE SACRED
# AND PROFANE

NOR MAY I LISTEN TO HIM WHO REASONS NOT UPON MY DEATH.*

Out of the forest, into the bright light bestowed by a
smile of eyes benign—what mortal mood is this,
what bitter sense of death? Why does death alone
seem company to love, why must the world be fled,
and why the chains and the renouncement? To ro-
mantic lovers, whose love despairs of anything but
mystic fusion, death is the one attainment left for
love; it is the blackness of the woods returning, filled
with uncertain spasms and distant tremors, and the
remote fanfare of the king's hunt. Eternal night without a shape or shore, such is love's own and sacred
indistinction: and the beloved face is of the shades
of night. For total fusion knows no freedom, will, or

---

* *Nè mi lece ascoltar chi non ragiona
della mia morte.*
(Francesco Petrarca—*Canzoniere*)

25

gods—only the blind compulsion of deep primeval darkness.

Of another death speaks the humanistic poet, a willing death, a sacrifice, a servitude of love. No more fears of darkness, nor blowing winds of hell: but waters clear, green meadows, and light of days serene. Though even here, in the shades of laurels, a death lies hidden, like a snake amid flowers and grass.

It was woman, indeed, who brought the world out of the black northern forests, peopled by monsters and sullen hierarchies. The damsel had waited for many a century upon her reef, guarded by feudal dragons, pining for the bold warrior who would come and break her chains: him, in turn, she made a free man. Troubadours of Provence and poets of the *Dolce Stil Nuovo,* the sweet new style, had placed her on the altars, the star and goddess of their rhymes: but the burden of their songs was the human and the free, and not the divine. Barbarous male gods gave way before the smiling Grace: the tongues were loosened and freed from religious reverence, changing their accents and sounds. Femininity's advent had given the world a new dimension, a perspective which renovated thought and syntax, language and paint-

ing. The greatest of revolutions was flourishing, like
all revolutions, under a benign female deity. Europe
returned to womanhood; and the deity's signs were,
in truth, nothing but memories from the former days
of feudal gods. Free courts of love were superseding
the cruel courts of lords, and retaining solely their
name and ceremonial; and it is singular that "court-
ship," "courting," "courtesy," derive from the usages of male and heroic times. The sacred hierarchies
of vassalage come to an end when amorous vassalage
is chosen. The inarticulate yell of hunter-kings gives
way to feminine speech and human sweetness. Who
could

> For such a wild and barbarous delight
> Forsake the ladies' pleasurable light? *

Thereafter, even the memory vanishes of the old
gods, and love profane runs free and sensual in the
cities and through the fields, where the priest of Var-
lungo, amid chestnuts and onions new, lies with fair
Monna Belcolore.** Free are the tongues, not hidden
any more in the obscurity of sacred Latin; free the

---

\* *per una sì selvaggia dilettanza*
  *lasciar le donne a lor gaia sembianza?*
  (Dante Alighieri—*Rime*)
\*\* From Boccaccio's *Decamerone.*

27

pursuits of commerce, no longer shameful nor forbidden, but open now to every Christian; free are the arts and crafts from Byzantine indifference; free, the relations between men, from symbols, hierarchies and serfdom. And man felt evermore inclined to a personal separate life, to a world impelled by interests and ambitions, resting entirely upon earth, and without gods. However, after the first happy flowering of a creative and impassioned liberty, Italian society broke up into a thousand distinct atoms, partaking no more in the sacred community, but intent with barren appetite of life, upon the merchant's endeavors, the interests of cold reason and the exercise of love. Thence, an impression of void and of peril—and also, from too much liberty, a sense of precariousness and the dread of happiness itself. From these vague and human fears new religions were taking shape—be it that the new lords and masters were reasserting the sacred nature of their strength, or that men of letters and artists were idolizing beauty, so that Giotto and Boccaccio, the most free of spirits, already show the first Latin signs of the coming academies. And man, who had found himself again, himself and his woman, feels the need of excluding her, once more, and of making her a

28

goddess—for the burden of an uncertain liberty
weighs upon him. No more a generical goddess of
womanhood, Beatrix of freedom and felicity; but a
particular divinity, with a name all her own, with
her own eyes and hair and face. And, being a deity,
she is a stranger and enemy:

So fierce was she, this enemy of mine,
And her I saw, her very heart was wounded. *

Not freedom any more, but religion is now the
basis for relationship with the adored enemy, and
her we owe the sacrifice of self. This is the way to
servitude of love, a willing servitude in the beginning:

Then did I wander, when the ancient gates
Of liberty were shut and locked before me

. . . . . . . .

Free at the start upon the path of sorrow
Yet now, alas, in bondage to another
Must go my soul, which sinnèd only once. **

---

* era si forte la nemica mia
  e lei vid' io ferita in mezzo 'l core.
  (F. Petrarca—Canzoniere)
** allora errai quando l'antica strada
   di libertà mi fu precisa e tolta

. . . . . . .

There is an initial sin—idolatry. But this sin once accepted, the servitude and death which ensue are only natural, for they alone confirm Laura's divinity, while giving truth and certainty to love. It is a wandering, a meandering through labyrinths, a failure to recognize one's own face, a renouncement of world and life, a continuous self-offering, a will to die, which save, however, both the idol and the believer, and which become eternal law and sacred scripture to the new religion of love. Without such religion, the thousand rites and interdictions, the spell of servitude and enchantment, would have no meaning—and they have none, indeed, in the unspeakable vortex of sacred love, and none in the pure sensuousness of love profane, and none in free love's creative comprehension. Weariness of liberty, unsatisfied senses, fear of the indistinctness of human communion generate the religion of love. And despite the tears and the wailing, sacrifice seems a lesser evil than the peril of freedom in the midst of passion:

Sighing for that which never would return

*allor corse al suo mal libera e sciolta*
*ora a posta d'altrui convien che vada*
*l'anima, che peccò solò una volta.*
(F. Petrarca—*Canzoniere*)

I said: The burden and the chains of serfdom
Were sweeter than this wandering alone. *

Petrarch, this greater Cézanne, under the same
skies of Provence, was feeling and summing up the
days of liberty gone by and the needs of the new
religion: needs of the inmost soul, entirely human
terrors, idolatrous quest of salvation.

This historical experience, which we find mani-
festing itself throughout the centuries and made eternal in art, is equal to the single experience of every
man in its various phases, and in the various aspects
of each phase. Sacred love, in its limitless power, is
anarchy and does not allow any act, but solely a
need, indefinite and lethal: such love cannot turn to
any particular woman, but only dwell in its own self,
in this chaotic oneness from which it proceeds and to
which it tends to return. This unbounded potency is
impotence. Here man is panting to be one with
woman, with all women, in the entirety of an undifferentiated sexuality, in the complete surrender of
fusion: the lover is unable to tell himself from his

---

* onde più volte sospirando indietro
dissi: Ohimè! il giogo e le catene e i ceppi
eran più dolci che l'andare sciolto.
(F. Petrarca—Canzoniere)

31

love or to set amorous bounds to the person beloved. And therefore, the gods of this terror must be themselves sexually indeterminate and double, or conversely—excessively male and female. Hence, in the most ancient mythologies, hermaphrodite and mutable deities coexist with other gods, consisting entirely of sex, erection and orgasm. The essential rite of these religions is *castration*, and, in a more civilized way, chastity—or the measureless blind embraces in the temples of India and Egypt, of Phoenicia and Syria, which correspond, in an opposite sense, to castration and chastity.

Circumcision may also be considered, from this point of view, as an equivalent for castration—and one should not be astonished at this additional meaning: each of these ritual acts may really have an infinite number of coexisting meanings, for infinite, also, are the terrors and the gods.

In order to know that these ambiguous deities, which are both day and night, summer and winter, sun and moon, man and woman, compel us to the sacrifice of abstinence and castration—each of us need only look inside himself. Blushing cheeks are evidence enough, without resorting to the thousands of observations made by psychiatrists and biologists, to the thousands of novels and tragedies which tell with infinite variety of moods the same romance of sacred terror and religious sacrifice. The impotence peculiar to youth is a religious defense against a premature communion, which would mean the loss of self. If a person has not yet acquired a distinct shape, how could he possibly unite with another one without melting away, or even perceive the other one's existence? Love and liberty are born together.

All things considered, sacred love is an impossibility: it leads to death even before the start. Such love, made religion, prevents its own fulfilment and thus procures salvation from that death. A voiceless abyss where all seeds are mingled, a shoreless sea which no eye may behold, a crossing from which no living soul ever returns—this is sacred love: deep black waters.

Nevertheless, in these waters, somebody is preening himself and smiling at himself, somebody who is everybody: Narcissus. Man is not yet adult; he is not free enough to recognize the *other*: but the need of love is born already, a need which makes one's own self appear as the other, and which turns inward the groping of desire. Inside, where there is nothing but waters and depth, Narcissus thinks to find another

33

self, responding to his smile, another self which may
be loved as an equal, and not dreaded like a woman
or a god. But this other one is merely an image, an
aerial fantasy—and this embrace too, is mortal.

Narcissus has always existed, even before the
Greeks made him into a graceful myth: he is eternal.
But the time which truly fits him best is that in which
a vital yearning for liberty and love is thwarted or
not yet fully grown: therefore, the seventeenth century, the *seicento*, lifts the sign of Narcissus upon its
banners in Caravaggio's style, and reacts to the
Counter-Reformation by shrinking into its own self,
by retiring into its innermost depth, mirrored in the
sensuous curves of the baroque. This was a time like
our own, of prisons and youthful solitude:

> From my solitudes I come,
> To my solitudes I go,
> For, to stay with my own self,
> My thoughts are company enough.*

---

* *de mis soledades vengo*
*a mis soledades voy*
*porqué, para estar con migo*
*me bastan mis pensamientos.*
(Lope de Vega)

Not in this solitude, still anarchical, but in another and democratic one, in the midst of the numberless crowd, stands the man who is too grown up, who is entirely segregated, limited and individual, entirely out of touch with the indefinite common, deprived of sacred powers and sacred terrors, and living without freedom and without gods. Others are present, of course, but inaccessible, because there no longer exists the tie that could unite them in mutual comprehension. Human relations are wholly external, and very easy, because they are non-existent. Modesty, restraint, truthfulness, chastity, impotence make no sense any more, and there are no more interdictions, or servitude, except the bonds of interest and usage. Even reality is gone; profane love is no love, and it does not lead to a death only because it proceeds from a death. Miserable are the triumphs of the individual:

> Old ones also are his pleasure
> For the boast of a full measure . . .*

---

* *delle vecchie fa conquista*
  *pel piacer di porle in lista*
  (Lorenzo Da Ponte—Libretto of Mozart's *Don Juan*)

35

until the terror of his own barrenness drives him again into idolatry. One single and definite woman becomes the goddess of a private cult; and rarely indeed does she attain, by grace of poetry, the level of the divine. Servitude of love requires its own rites and mutilations, its own hatreds and wars: to nurture his idol, the worshipper must give his life away, while wounding and despising the deity itself. The rite that fits this religion of love is *sadism*: without the double sacrifice of self and of the idol beloved, worship vanishes and love is possible no more. Hence, the offences and injuries, the deceits and lies and blows, the mortifications and murders. A definite person is made sacred, because of her very definiteness and limitation: the entire world, therefore, must shrink to these limits, must lose its freedom and universality, and become this single object of love. In this confined horizon and idolatrous wretchedness, in the sweetness of these chains, the narrower the space in the accepted prison, the more one feels inclined to totally adore. In such a drying up and shriveling of the soul every self-inflicted mutilation seems holy, every humiliation and abasement acceptable in order to reach a complete religious fixation. Circe, the divine magician, goes on and on eternally taking from her adorers their likeness of men and turning them into beasts, into dogs and swine; and they, barking and grunting, express their joy and delight.

As the worshipper offers to his deity the sacrifice of his own human nature, so the idol itself must also be sacrificed: and it is a true idol only if downtrodden, offended, restricted, diminished. Not only does the beloved forsake her quality as a person, but even her appearance and the integrity of her shape—shrinking to a material part, to a leg, to a head of hair, to a breast, to a gown, to a mere object. And the love focused upon this object turns into a cruel revenge for all that has been lost. Even further than that: the idol-object ceases to have any connection with the person beloved, and becomes a fetishistic symbol, one of the thousands which psychoanalysts have so carefully classified. The more limited and precise and corporeal this symbolic object, the greater its divine potency: a glove, a picture, an excrement become irresistible, irreplaceable amorous deities, absolute tyrants.

Thus, in the private and tender and daily field of love, we are confronted with the same vicissitudes as in the field of the relationship between man and the

37

state. Outside the freedom of a person completed, able therefore to conceive the other, to identify itself with the other in a common human nature, there is nothing but a sacred death in primeval indistinction, or a death profane in barren distinctness. Between the two impossible opposites of sacred love and love profane, any attempt at religious salvation is nothing but castration or sadism, puritanism or libertinage, extremes born of one single process. Between these two coincident extremes forever oscillate religious lovers. It is the old problem of spirit and body, which have contended since the very inception of time. The historical transition between the reign of the *Roi Soleil* and the Regency, or between the Victorian era and Lawrence's priapic revolution, is taking place continually and without hope of salvation in every man, incapable of freedom, who has made of his affections an idol, and offered sacrifices and offered up his self.

Love is not only the elementary human relationship, the first discovery of the world, the touchstone of liberty, it is also procreation, family, and therefore society and state. The point of interest here is not how love may exist, but how it may serve the greater deities of the fathers, of the clan, the tribe, the state. And certainly it is love, in its free and individual nature, which must be sacrificed to these gods. When the father is god, there is no room for love: woman is a slave, not an equal. The gravest offence is adultery, solely because it means a betrayal of God (jealousy is a divine sentiment, an impious deed, a siding with the enemy, with a stranger, with another god. Therefore, the adulterous woman is sacred, deserving of death, untouchable. Only a god son, who does not know of foreign deities, can look upon her with pity, and send her home alive. The father chooses brides for his sons, and sells his daughters as mere commodities. Jacob finds in his bed a woman he does not want, and pays with seven years of servitude for the wife of his choice, thus rendering homage to the divine authority of his father Laban: and only as a girl in love could Laban's daughter, portending a more exalted God, steal for love's sake the deities of the father, humble herself in hiding them, and sit upon them, in the camel's saddle.

For the tribe, ancient or modern, that worships not a familiar but a collective god, women are common property: adultery and sacrilege is only that which is committed outside the tribe, there where another sacred animal holds its sway. In the tribe too, but even more so in the paternal state, women have no gods of their own, and are ruled solely by the deities of their menfolk. Women may therefore be ravished by the foe, and even if born at home, they always remain strangers, because they take part in the rites only as victims. Love is impossible when it is thus turned into servitude. What counts is not the certitude of love, but that of matrimony, of children, of the family. Woman is sacrificed to the father-god. The mythical founders of cities have no human father; they are the sons of gods, of sacred virgins, of animals. They never could have separated from a true father to establish another patrician city-state: therefore their birth must be mysterious. So that Jesus might speak of love, he had to be a son without a father—and his voice truly opened locked doors. But the divine fathers and the divine States live eternally, and jealously claim, throughout eternity, the slavery of woman and the sacrifice of love.

# IV.

## SLAVERY

Admission into Oriental and Grecian mysteries was gained through the initiation of sacrifice. Fasting, abstinence, purification, chastity, mutilations, macerations, renouncement of love or modesty were the indispensable preliminaries, and perhaps the mystery which the believer could then behold was nothing but a sacred pageant, where the same sacrifices were performed by the gods; a symbolic performance, revealing the symbol, but not the symbol's meaning, which remained, even to the initiated, mysterious in its multiplicity, ambiguous and infinite, like terror and like the gods themselves. All the interpretations, from the grossest to the most sublime, which are rediscovered with such learned ingenuity to explain these ancient rites, may be quite true, but none of them is satisfactory: because, in truth, the rite resolved itself into the symbol and did not require explanation. The mortal vagueness, from which escape was sought, resided not in reason, but in feeling—and therefore the symbolic liberation had to be perceived through feeling, not through reason. A voluntary servitude gives birth to the idols; it is by itself an initiation; it breaks away from the worlds both of indeterminate and of personal life, and thus creates another world, where life is ritual, a world most truly powerful when evident in its appearance and mysterious in its meaning.

The life of every single individual, and the entire history of mankind, taken as a religious history and life, may be considered as one great mystery, in which every man and every historical period gain admission and initiation at every moment, in each fraction of time. It is a mystery, obscure to reason, but crystal clear to religious feeling, which seeks only a limited, perceptible, evident certitude. And this mystery, this history, is one eternal sacrifice, which alone enables the weirdness of myth to change into the mysterious certainty of ritual. The horrid darkness of night swarms, for the child, with monsters which still seem frightful only because they fail to take a definite shape: but imagining monsters is already an attempt

at religious liberation. The discovery of women—
an unutterable incertitude—turns into tyranny, fet-
ishism, sadism; the darkness of family communion
turns into patriarchy. Even man's relation to his own
creative powers is made certain and definite through
idolatry: creation becomes *work*, a malediction from
heaven. Language itself loses its vital and poetical
meaning, and tends to become symbolical, evocative
and magical, confining itself to clear formulations,
full of practical power and devoid of meaning:

> . . . Speak lower, Mnasylus: the gods
>     are everywhere,
> Hecate's eye divine is gleaming from
>     the dark.*

says the Parnassian poet. But how can we hide,
when every action of ours, every word, is a deity?

Eternal renouncement, ceaselessly renewed, nur-
tures the idol and is itself an idol, connecting the
image of the past with that of the future by a tie
which seems historical and is in fact religious. In
this way, individual life finds continuity through a

---

*. . . *Parle bas, les dieux sont partout, ô Mnasyle,*
*Hécate nous regarde avec son oeil divin*
(José-Maria de Hérécha)

continuous self-denial, and man makes of his own self a stranger and a victim.

That which goes for the individual applies also to society and to the state. The state-idol can exist only through a process of social alienation and sacrifice: only through *slavery*. Slavery and divineness of the state are exactly the same: the divine nature of the state is slavery, and slavery could not exist without the state's divinity, for deity and victim coincide.

The civilizations of antiquity, where the state rests upon religion, are based upon slavery, derive their origin from slavery, and would not be conceivable without it: in vain do moralists and philosophers deplore the fact of slavery as a disgrace, as a blemish upon the face of an otherwise heavenly star. True, these civilizations are not exclusively religious; but their state organization is founded on a religious world. Slavery is therefore an absolutely inseparable and essential element of their structure. Hence, all the movements of servile rebellion are doomed to failure: in no mythology were gods ever overthrown and struck down by victims—only by fearless, innocent or wise men. Giants may scale Olympus and dark angels storm the skies: but they are confined within the world which they have accepted, which is theirs, without which they would not exist—and the gods can smile at their revolt. Spartacus naturally falls—because his rebellion is absurd as long as he clings to a slave's banner and recognizes implicitly both slavery and the divinity of the state. This is the necessary fate of all movements of revolt in which the victim objects to the knife, but not to the altar; the fate of every attempt (however humanely legitimate) which starts as a demand for liberation, that is, for abstract justice, and not for liberty itself. For the state-idol, the institution of slavery is vital law, and therefore concrete justice. The revolt of the slaves may at most lead to a reversal of functions; it may, as in some imaginary drawing by Goya, turn the goat into the sacrificer. This is, as we shall see, the true weakness of those proletarian movements which not without reason have fondly called themselves by the ill-omened name of Spartacism; and, generally, the weakness of all those movements, be they of ever so radical an appearance, which do not step beyond the religious limits of the civilization they try to supersede.

For the state to be a god, man in his entirety, man the essence of state, must become enslaved; and all men are enslaved, from the king to the meanest pariah. To be precise, as long as there is one single slave, everybody shares his servitude. However, sacrifice being a symbol, universal servitude must be symbolized by somebody in particular, somebody whose specific function is, for all men's sake, to take this servitude upon himself, to display it ostensibly, to become for all men a stranger to the state, and for all men the victim. In an organic state, the institution of slavery is a *necessary* organ, the one which allows the other organs to enjoy some relative freedom. Not only the patricians and plebeians, but also the slaves, first of all the slaves, should have been mentioned in the famous fable by Menenius Agrippa about the irreplaceable members of the social body—and he did not mention them perhaps because they are sacred and therefore unmentionable; or maybe the metaphor was not a happy one, because they are the parts of a divine, not of a human body.

Who therefore, as a consecrated victim, shall bear upon his shoulders the divinity of the state? Who shall support the state without being a part of it? Evidently, the strangers: those who are of alien origin as well as those who become alien by exercising a function considered as fitting the aliens: conversely, the activity of strangers shall appear as a

46

servile occupation. Foreign men and foreign things, more than all the others, seem to be of a divine quality; by their very nature, by the very fact of their strangeness and hostility, they are sacred things, to be sacrificed.

In warlike states, whose gods are gods of battle, the slaves become first of all the prisoners. Slaves fit for sacrifice, to be slaughtered on the altars, or to be kept alive, in order to perform those functions that are strange to the military state: the general functions of manual and mechanical work, which for the warrior are disgraceful, and therefore sacred; and also the more peculiarly disgraceful functions of the so-called infamous occupations, sometimes including commerce, and even medicine and philosophy. These were, approximately, the functions of the slaves in Rome. Because of their existence, the plebe was never comparable to the modern proletariat or a lower class; it was a kind of middle class, which, although it had to struggle for centuries before gaining full rights and transforming patrician law into a citizens' law, was never entirely in bondage. The existence of slavery allowed for relative plebeian liberty, and the freedom of civil struggles. It also allowed the union between the warrior gods of the

47

fathers and the rustic gods of the most ancient Italians; the fusion (which has never been complete) of two quite different trends; the original grafting of a military, state-worshipping, religious, juridical civilization upon a rustic civilization which was anarchical, irreligious and poetical. Here we may find the reason why Roman expansionism was a necessity: the freedom of Rome's citizens required an ever growing servitude. The fertile civil struggles could develop only with the help of foreign wars: so that Rome might be free, the entire world had to fall into slavery.

Where slaves cannot be captured in war, or bought for money, in states which are self-contained, weak or pacific, the citizens themselves must be enslaved, through a process of expulsion and differentiation. Castes, closed guilds and hierarchy are born. In Egypt, a country of cities and sedentary agriculture, dependent upon the river and the seasons, the lowest caste was considered as the most foreign: the nomads, the swineherds and shepherds. In the Oriental fables, sorceresses turn the prince into a swineherd, the last degree of human slavery. The wandering Hebrews were slaves, both as strangers and as herdsmen.

The castes of India result from the crystallizing of

an extremely complex history; they are bred by a
religiosity which is more social then political. The
Indian state is nothing but an idol of the very hierarchy of bondage. In the overflowing sacred and
corresponding religiousness, every action, every relation, every contact becomes impossible and forbidden. Closed worlds living in mutual ignorance
coexist in infinite numbers, like the infinity of the
gods. Each has its own interdictions, each is shameful and untouchable for the others. Here the religion of human relationship, born of the incumbent
fear of confusion, has destroyed the state, turning it
into a dead impossibility.

The history of the Hebrews, considered as a sacred
history, or rather, as a mythology (and we are not
dealing here with their religious and profane history,
which is that of a small Oriental people incessantly
struggling between transcendency and idolatry), ne-
gates every idol that is an enemy of the Lord. The
entire people had been slaves in Egypt and were to be
slaves in Babylon, and again in times to come: a
voluntary servitude, for they had sacrificed to the
idols. But after they gain faith in the transcendent
God, which is not a god of human relations, that is—
after they renounce every state-idolatry, the people

49

are no longer the slaves of men. They shall be only the servants of God, "for unto me the children of Israel are servants; * they are my servants whom I brought forth out of the land of Egypt," (that is—of idolatry) "and they shall not be sold as bondsmen." ** They have no state, they do not live tied to the earth, "for the land is mine, for ye are strangers and sojourners with me." *** Thus, there cannot be slavery upon earth: but the people, eternally foreign to the earth, are chosen to be the servants and victims of divine transcendency.

After the transformation of the Roman republic— a people's republic and city-state—into an Empire embracing all the nations of the known world, the time was ripe for Christian preaching, which extended the gift of election to all men and tried to sever them, in matters of faith, from the earthly fathers and from every idol of state and society. Moreover, the classical form of Roman slavery, whose institutions were characteristic of a military state, at once aristocratic and popular, was bound to fall into decay after the consolidation of the monarchy. Slav-

---

* Leviticus, XXV, 55.
** Leviticus, XXV, 42.
*** Leviticus, XXV, 23.

ery was becoming softer, its limits were now easy to cross; the right of citizenship, formerly almost unobtainable, because it entailed participation in the divinity of the state, could now be acquired with more ease; and this is only logical, because citizenship, that is the divinity of the city, as well as slavery in its traditional form, which provides victims for the paternal deities and later for the city-gods, was gradually losing its value and significance. As long as family gods were in power, gods of patrician nobility, gods of city and society, these particular deities required particular victims, and slavery therefore embraced everything which was strange to the clan's nobility and the city's tradition. Under the deified monarch, the state being gathered in *one,* the ancient slavery, manifold and particular, loses its meaning. Under the king, everybody is a servant: the unity of the idol requires the totality of the victims. This explains how slavery, which had been within precise limits a well-defined institution of the state, becomes under the Empire a fundamental principle permeating the entire state—so that the loosening of the former bonds of slavery entails the loss of every personal and civic freedom. The state becomes orientalized; society is turning into a mass

51

without shape or limits. The idolatrous reverence for the state is growing stronger, and every single man, unable to be a member of the body politic, an active and effective bearer of the entire polity, turns to the only possible participation, to the last means by which to avoid the loss of every human relationship, and becomes a worshipper, a servant and victim of the state. Total servitude has to be organized; the castes originate, in which the common ritual of devotion to the state is allowed to combine with a thousand other particular rites of social devotion. Thus, upon the ruins of former liberty and former slavery, the guilds come to life; and they are born with the hallmark of trade—which alone differentiates the members of a shapeless mass—and with the sign of the sepulchre, with the sign of the religion of the dead, which alone attempts salvation from the eternal dissolving indistinctness.

The return of barbarism has really nothing in common with primitive barbarism, for there always endures in it a feeling for the singleness of the state, despite the infinite multiplicity of states; and thus there coexist with the numberless dragons and lions, horses and monsters of barbarism, the eagles of empire, these solitary oceanic birds; with the numberless feudal and particular servitudes, the general and terrestrial bondage to the Holy Empire; and the celestial bondage to the only god is not forgotten, despite the existence of innumerable minor deities, of countless relics, all of them holy. Thus, while men still believe in one God, wars are waged to deprive the foe of the gods they adore, of their saintly relics, of their idols, and therefore of their particular freedoms. Thus, slavery is simultaneously a general principle, underlying the common hierarchic life, and a particular institution, connected with each single god. In other words, all men are servants, in a greater or lesser measure, to the only king: but, as the various deities have returned to the soil, to the woods of the hunter, deep down to the ground, the servants of servants have become the serfs of the soil. The tilling of fields, the most human of toils, is strange to an earth which is divine in its savage nature, in its naked powers, and which is subdivided not according to the varying cultures and crops, but solely according to limits set by the violent rule of some heraldic beast. Therefore, the labor of fields is the labor of serfs, victims of an earth which has again become sacred. And not only work in the fields, but work in general is foreign to these gods of violence and honor—work

53

which in times religious and sacred cannot but remind us of a time more human and anticipate future
days of freedom. Particularly commerce is strange
to these gods, which are tied to the earth, to a piece of
earth the size of whatever their falcon-eyes may be
able to encompass, or of whatever may extend under
the walls of the castle. What men are these, obstinate
against the times, attempting to infuse the lifeblood
of economy into a crystallized world, and creating
contacts between secluded lands, without roads, each
with its own local god, lordly self-sufficient? Their
activity is foreign to the new religious civilization; it
is therefore a sacred and contemptible activity, privileged and subject to arbitrary taxation. In the feudal
civilization there is no place but that of a victim for
the merchant—and commerce, not without reason, is
an achievement of the Jews, of this people without
idols, perforce strangers to escutcheons, to emblems
and to gods. It was a necessity that such a foreign
people should exist, to carry on an activity which,
however necessary, was incompatible with the deities
of fountains and lakes, of forests and castles: it was
necessary that custom and law should render this
people more and more explicitly foreign, that they
should segregate its members in the most radical

manner and oppose every attempt at fusion, that they should exclude them from humanity, so that their necessary function would not offend those sedentary gods, those gods of strongholds whose task it was to firmly establish the nests and boundaries, the limits and interdictions of a world which had grown to be limitless, boundless and open. Serfs bound to the furrow, like crawling animals, *animaux rampants,* as they appeared to La Bruyère; or merchants of a people made strangers to men, (or belonging to the republics of seafarers, for the fluid gods of the sea are quite unlike the gods of forests and hills): necessary mutilations, inevitable sacrifices, giving life to the thousand new gods of feudal hierarchy, which were to save mankind from the terror of a new sacred confusion.

A confusion of rights and peoples, of races and nations and languages and gods; a universal return to the sacred silence of shapelessness, such is the meaning of the Roman Empire in the period usually described as that of its decline and fall. The frontiers extended to the limits of the world, the many languages merged in one, all the peoples mixed together, all the powers concentrated in a single point, and the fullness of servitude weighing upon all—the

55

world of men was returning to its first state of a chaotic mass, sacred, ineffable, undifferentiated. Ancient slavery had lost its meaning, for it was an
articulate slavery, a class slavery, indispensable for
the freedom of other classes. Similarly, all the gods
of antiquity were fading away, merging their respec-
tive attributes and rituals, since the particular fears
and the particular needs of liberation from which
they were born were dissolving into the unity of a
new terror. This sacred reflowering engulfed the ancient traditions of countries grown old as well as the
fresh impulses of barbarian newcomers. Idle were the
attempts at restoring the deities of old—classical
polytheism was reaching its end amid the anguishing
indistinctness of a limitless world, of a nameless and
speechless mass, of a vague mysterious forest. Feudal
religion, by creating a new slavery and a new privilege, was again dividing the forest according to certain boundaries and giving the world an iron frame
to prevent its disintegration; feudalism was driving
out a part of man so that life might continue, and
circumcising itself in order to gain consecration.
The symbols of the countless new gods, the rites of
the numberless new victims were creating new religious languages, and thus giving mankind a new

*practical* means of expression. Until the day of liberty's return (return as a fundamental and visible element of civil life, for naturally, neither in man nor in mankind had liberty ever entirely disappeared): a day when freedom would create new languages, a new ideal perspective, a new culture and a new poetry.

# V.

# THE MUSES

With the dissolving of the Roman world into an imperial society essentially inorganic, the Latin language also dies and disappears. That a language, the one language of an entire world, spoken by every people under every sky, should by and by become incomprehensible and empty, and grow into a thousand shapes of baby talk, may seem a miracle, but not a greater one than each man's daily aging and continuous rebirth.

The world of the Empire, in its universal servitude, in its colossal uniformity, deprived human relations of all their freedom, and despoiled them of every particular religion: there was no place any more for the person, but only for a single shapeless mass, and the altars stood empty, stripped of the old gods. It

was vain, then as always, to turn back: the philosophers and politicians who sought for the lost freedom
in a society and in a cult which were already dead,
could place it only in the abstract individual, in his
virtue and conscience; and these philosophers were
turning into noble statues of salt, stoically barren.
Their Latin therefore became a secret language, understood by the initiated only.

But the shapeless mass, the initial human chaos, is
speechless. Its unity is pure inexpressible power.
Every word is implicit therein, all languages merged
in confusion—but nothing can be uttered: a single
spoken word would open the dark womb. Therefore
the ancient Latin tongue withdraws from the lips as
well as the thoughts, and the open clarity of expression gives way ever more to a human silence, full
of every terror and every possibility.

Not from the abstract profoundness of the individual conscience, nor from bright stoical virtue are
born the new gods, but from another depth: from the
depth of the earth, and from the glitter of arms. Latin
remained the sacred language of a divinity imperial
and dead. New gods were shaping new religious languages, but at the same time, as the mass was differ-

59

entiating, and freedom dimly dawning again, new poetical languages were also coming to life.

There exists a religious language, which at first may be a mute language, consisting of signs, of attitudes; in a family religion it is made up of names and possessions, in a feudal religion, of fiefs, coats of arms, badges, banners, weapons, usages, impositions, manumissions, declarations, and so forth. There is also a religious language which is spoken and figurative, made up of sacred images and of prayers. And finally, the entire language, inasmuch as it has a symbolic and not an expressive value, is a religious language; every word contains in itself a god, and, eternally true to itself, represents the god and turns it into an object. Religion is the individuating limitation of that which has no shape, the symbolical fixation of the indeterminate. Religion's expression always refers to something that is beyond it, to a transcendent deity or to a deified object which always remains outside the symbol. Religious language is therefore inexpressive by its very nature. A prayer should not make any sense; a prayer is more efficacious when pronounced in a dead language or in a language which is not understood: however, like every symbol, a prayer must be precise, well defined, and capable of infinite repetition. Its aim is not the creation of thought, but of certainty. Such is the entire language of heraldry: insignia and banners do not represent the fief or the nation, but they are the sign of the fief's and nation's certainty and divineness.

Religious language has no value in itself, but only in relation with the object symbolized: therefore this language must be together inexpressive and perfectly clear. Playing cards are perfect religious images: quite rightly, therefore, are they used for drawing lots and divining the future.

Religious language originates from a need of fixation and certitude. The religious images or words, in their limitation, take the place of a frightful reality—and they must be capable of identical repetition, so as to free us, through their immutability, from that terrible changefulness which they come to replace. The crest makes the earl, the flag makes the nation, the cognomen makes the family, the uniform makes the army, the prayers make the god. They make him a certainty, a practical reality—not an image—a living reality which cannot be repeated.

Religious expression is therefore the contrary of poetical expression. The former is a symbolic lim-

61

itation of the universal, the latter—the concrete expression thereof; the one is the manifested certainty of a divine, liberating servitude, the other is the voice itself of human liberty; on the one hand—fixed ritual, on the other—mythology. Strictly speaking, one cannot ascertain a "before" and an "after," neither individually nor historically, between these two contradictory expressions—but only a complementary alternation. The child is born mute, and cannot speak as long as it remains an unlimited being, uncertain and chaotic: its cries are vague and impersonal like the rustling of leaves. But although its expressions are poetical or religious, according to its development as a person or its adherence to custom, and although, beneath the prevailing ritual (for the child's world is essentially religious) the personal myths, born of true facts or of the creative imagination, make their appearance—nevertheless, the child's first language consists in great part of magic formulas, endowed with great evocative and practical efficiency. The true live speech develops later on, with the maturing of the person, with the discovery of the world, which cannot be summoned up at the sound of a prayer, but which unfolds and takes shape through the warmth of love.

Art may be considered as a *mythology* (if by the word "myth" we mean the expression of a particular spiritual world), inasmuch as art should be referred to that element of feeling which conditions it, and which in it is merged and exhausted. Art is a totality, for both the element of indeterminateness and that of particularity originate there, and the abyss takes shape without losing depth, and passion expresses itself without howling, and man appears entire, unfettered, sufficient unto himself. Strictly speaking, there is no religious art: to say there is would be a contradiction in terms. Art resolves within itself, without residue, the entire moral and religious world, as well as the vague areas of sentiment and feeling. And, whenever religion is told in terms of poetical myth, it is mere poetry, and no longer religion. The Bible itself, as the mythology of the Hebrew people, is nothing but a work of art; it becomes a moral and theological code only when these myths are being severed from their particular and historical expression, from their peculiar and unique value —that is, when they are no longer interpreted as myths, but as symbols of a truth which lies outside them, and which, being eternally the same, renders them fit for eternal repetition. The live characters of

Tolstoy are myths of absolute happiness, of total youthful freedom: the others, who have no artistic reality, remain the symbols of a world of moral velleities. D. H. Lawrence's most convincing figures are myths of an eternal puritan struggle between body and soul—but they live, through their hopeless ventures and provisory solutions, in a manner which is unique; the other figures, artistically unsuccessful, give us the religious symbols of this struggle: a white bird, and a wooden turgidity. In other words, art creates myths even when its abstract content is religious; and religion believes in symbols, even when the world from which it arises is a world of freedom. Religious expression is a need of certainty—certainty not only of that which has no shape, but even of that which has form and life. Every word becomes religious when one thinks of it as possessing a value and a meaning *in itself*, as capable of remaining significant by itself—that is, as something which symbolizes another reality, permanent and transcendent, to which it is the magical key. Every rhythm, every rhyme turns into things religious whenever, instead of arising together with the verse, they are left to remain like a scaffolding, like an external sign of poetry. All language is inexpressively religious inasmuch as it serves to endow us through its symbols with a sure and practical means of contact, inasmuch as it serves to represent schematically our needs and actions, and, at the sacrifice of creativity, to give us the certitude of an external relationship, the feeling of a space and time extraneous to thought, and immutable. Finally, art is religious in its entirety when the living myths thereof become for the artist mere symbols of their own selves, as happens in every period marked by "the religion of Art," as well as in the life of every single artist. There follows an external artistic continuity, which is not so much a sign of the permanence of a certain personal world, as indeed an act of faith in certain forms grown symbolic and divine: an act by which one renounces the peril of creative freedom, and obtains—through sacrifice—a certainty. Most of an artist's changes, in style or period, are religious crises arising in some private artistic religion of his own: he needs to get rid of the old and dead symbols in order to create new myths and escape fixation.

Popular art is eminently religious, in all its forms —figurative, musical, architectural, poetical, as well as those that merge with habit, dress and custom, and with the thousand rites which accompany life. Popular art is simply the fixation and perpetuation of moods and means originally expressive, which have lost their former peculiar significance and turned into stereotyped and merely symbolic expressions. Not only the objects of popular devotion, such as fetishes, the statuettes of family-gods, the images endowed with miraculous powers, the figures of saints and Madonnas, the formulas of exorcism and magic, but even artistic objects with no perceivable religious content, such as the dolls, the obscene scribblings on walls, the songs and ditties of love, the traditional shapes given to loaves of bread and to other familiar things, the decorative sculptures of fountains, houses, utensils and tools, the ceremonials of cooking and eating, etc.—are nothing but symbols, where the only value resides in the certainty of the thing or idea represented, while the way of representing it is fixed, and therefore non-expressive and solely religious. It is precisely the sameness of the representation which confers to the latter its value and authority: it is the process of prayer and sacrifice. The fixity of style is the characteristic of popular art—as well as of children's art, if we are to believe Alain, who says that children live in a world peopled solely by gods.

Religious figuration and artistic expression are antithetical: the latter, a purely human creation, knows no other law than its own, implicit and eternally changeable, even when picturing the objects of religion; the former has the task of *relegating* art to the altar of certitude and duration, of relating and tying it to its own patterns, so that art may continue; of sacrificing it, so that it may become a symbolic tie and relation, and therefore a practical communication between men. The contrast is one of creation and limit. A positive religion is only in part a matter of religiosity; it may even lack any religious content, or it may contain it side by side with the more conspicuous political, historical or sentimental elements: to such a point, that a given religion may represent not so much a religiousness as an entire civilization—and this necessarily pervades the entire field of art. But the religious vision of the Sistine Chapel, of the *Divine Comedy*, of *Paradise Lost*, or of the *Promessi Sposi* * is merely the occasion for a new mythology, which cannot be repeated, and in which the religious motive disappears. Conversely, if religion be the power of limitation, wherein language changes into symbol and the freely created

* *The Betrothed*, by Manzoni.

world annuls itself in order to endure—then every artistic activity will appear in the guise of a drama, and its limits will be determined, as by a negative image, by the contours of religion itself. A negative image, reciprocal and reflected. We have all of us struggled until dawn with the Angel, and the Angel did not tell us his name (angels do not express themselves) : but this struggle has left its mark upon each of our works; as upon the hip of the Patriarch Jacob: the reflection of a religious vision.

The individual works of art which draw their inspiration from a religious "content" do not constitute in the least a religious art; rather are they an artistic liberation from the gods and the rites they depict. But in certain periods of history, where the ever-present horror of sacredness weighs upon men and compels them to take refuge behind the gods, a diffuse religiosity permeates the least expression, infiltrates the language and shapes it in its own fashion. When the sense of the world is placed outside the world, when every action and every thought are a sacrifice to a deity, language foregoes its autonomous creative value and assumes a symbolic signification. Every part of the language, every single sentence, every word in the sentence becomes a divine

symbol: and every symbol, every word has an absolute value, identical with every other, because all of
them equally contain and postulate a god. Every symbol must be entire and totally representative: every
word becomes valuable, and dwells in isolation.
Syntax dissolves: the single elements of a sentence acquire an equal importance, and equally suggestive
powers.

Under the compulsion of sacredness, in the ur-
ban forest of Rome and the black forest of Germany,
the world, turns into mass, becomes mute. The Latin
tongue disappears: but for a language, to become
mute means to undergo mutation. Meanwhile, as a
salvation from sacredness, deities arise in infinite
numbers and all life dries up in stony religious
forms, the new languages themselves are also filled
with religiousness, with servitude and interdictions—
and even syntax and phonetics are transformed to the
core. The one language, Latin, changes into the Romance, or new Latin, languages—according to the
particular spirit of the various peoples, who feel, in
front of that mortal limitless unity, an obscure need
of differentiation.

This linguistic mutation is interpreted by the phi-
lologists in terms of phonetics. If we take for instance

the formation and transformation of ancient French, the reason for it is sought in the overlong accent with two stresses, which is supposedly characteristic of the Celtic spirit, the Celtic element having merged with the Romanic. But how did it happen, asks Vossler, that this accent, in the first period of medieval French, until approximately the year 1050, led to progressive displacements, while in the second period it caused displacements which were regressive? Why do diphthongs appear first, and later on—monophthongs? First palatal, and later guttural displacements? First the assimilation, and then the loss of consonants? First the closed syllables, and later the open ones? First the consonantal, and then the vocalic ending of words? First the richness and later the poverty of the phonetic material and of the inflections? The reply, rightly says the German philologist, is to be sought in the style of the language. The diphthong arises when the tonic accents become too frequent, and they are frequent when the structure of speech is *paratactical.* * The monophthongs, on the contrary, predominate when the sentence has acquired a tonic balance, and a *syntactical* construc-

---

* *"Parataxis:* co-ordinative ranging of propositions one after another, without other expression of their syntactic relation (he laughed; she cried)." (Webster)

70

tion. And precisely, around the year 1050, both the phonetic and the syntactic mutations take place in medieval French, together with the general change in taste, culture, customs—together with the growth of a new, widespread freedom, and the progressive decay of feudal deities and religious ties.

The primitive expression, that of the world which arose directly from the fall of the Empire and of the Latin language, was an expression, as we have seen, imbued with religiosity. Its syntax, therefore, is para-tactical: every word, every image is closed in itself, complete, without ties, and equal in its value to every other one. The images, all equally symbolic, stand side by side, without correlation or opposition: discourse is a *mosaic*. The stress falls upon every word; all of them are on the same plane: there cannot be a *perspective*. Furthermore, as there is no syntactic relationship, every single word must contain in it-self the entire concept: inflections are abundant and complicated (dual number, third future tense, etc.).

These considerations about the phonetic expression are also valid with regard to the figurative expres-sions. Whenever, in a language, the inflections are complicated—in painting, a man viewed frontally shall have his face in profile. If stress falls equally

71

on every word all perspective shall be developed on a plane and described without relations; and the relative dimensions of objects are of no importance: a flower or a mountain are both the size of a man, equally symbolic, equally stressed. The greater the poverty of relationship, the richer, the more precious and complicated are the local values and the pictorial matter. When the construction is paratactical, the elements of the pictorial discourse can have, in a painting, only a symmetrical order. In poetry, where the verses are all of one measure, symmetry produces the rhyme, the primitive rhyme which is monotonous. Whereas in words every symbol must be complete in itself, which leads to the formation of diphthongs and consonantal groups of awkward pronunciation, similarly in pictures the gems and golden backgrounds jar side by side with every imaginable tone. The paratactical construction, the symbolic and religious value of expression are thus exalting symmetry and local color, while abolishing tonality and composition. The mosaic, which even materially, technically, is paratactical, becomes the preferred technique.

The art of these Primitives is therefore the art of absolute authority; it has the same characteristics as the Romance languages in their first, early medieval period, the ritual, symbolical, divine period.

The weakening of religiousness through the growth of a sense of humanity, through the liberation of love, through the disappearance of monsters and terrors and the dissolution of hell, creates modern values, modern freedom, modern syntaxes and perspective and languages. The *Dolce Stil Novo*, the sweet novel style of early Italian literature, and the painters before Giotto—including Cimabue and Duccio—mark this crisis: Dante and Giotto are at its highest summit, at the powerful whirlwind where intermingle the clashing trends of feudal religion and of liberty. But Masaccio and Boccaccio (these two extraordinary names of disparagement, the one for Thomas, the doubter who touches, * the other for the mouth, the most human of our organs, since its function is speech) are already entirely engaged *in partibus infidelium*. The ugly is chosen, out of passion for that which is alive; there is no more gold; Latinized prose flows like a stream, involved and syntactical. And if a new religion is born therefrom, it is purely literary religion, a religion of art, mother of academies, of courtly speech, of beautifully inex-

* The Gospel, John XX, 24–29.

pressive painting—of all that, alas, which in Italy is usually called the Italian "tradition." But one well understands the enthusiasm of a Paolo Uccello for the discovery of perspective: a liberated world, where everything was relationship, believed it had found the very secret of its liberty. The spiked collar of Paolo Uccello* was only a myth—which all too soon became a material symbol in the new worship of perspective, in the architectonic canon of sixteenth-century painting.

The forms of expression in the first period of medieval art were permeated with religious spirit, as we have learned from the language and art of the time. The expressive shapes of the next period, on the contrary, were full of the sense of freedom. These statements should not be understood in a materialistic way—for evidently every work of art, even in the oldest period, was also a work of free creation, the translation into myths of that religious world from which it arose; by the same token, every work of art in the later period was the happy myth of its own free world. In the most primitive period, poetry could originate only from a contrast with the spirit

* Famous drawing, made according to the laws of mathematical perspective.

of the time, and was perforce dramatic, and rare as grass in a desert. It was a time of prayer for a humanity that had to gain salvation from the terror of the millennium; and prayer, upon the lips of the cleric and the brush of the painter, came naturally, for the sake of the world's continuance, to make sure that human speech should not be silenced, that it should not cease to be understood, like the tongue of the Giants. This unconscious urge acted like a tremendous drive, giving its sense to every expression. In the following period, the sense was that of poetry, the feeling of a world renewed, which had forgotten the gods and now considered them unnecessary and hostile; a world which was disentangling itself, through the infinitely various liberty of creation, from the shackles and the serfdom of the fathers. These secret currents which give a tonality to an entire epoch, and which are in every man the same, (for all men are driven to avoid the plunge into the sacred, as well as severance from it), are much deeper than that which in the field of art has come to be called "taste." They are that dark necessity which creates differences and frees from dissolution, that necessity through which life endures beyond serfdom and blasphemy and death, until it shines in liberty again; that which makes art painful and contradictory and often partial and miscarrying in times of religion, and which causes the happy art of free times. Therefore is it vain to force upon religion the merit of that which we may call the genius or the feeling or the taste ("the Taste of the Primitives") of a certain period in history. In medieval art, "taste" was at first religious and anti-artistic, and later on poetical and anti-religious. In other times, more recent, and also considered as primitive, the opposite process prevailed: impressionism, the power of freedom, came first, followed later by the returning urge of religiousness. If one can speak of taste, or of genius, or of the general artistic feeling displayed by a certain period, it is precisely because the spirit of the time pervades every organ and form of expression, so that language and art may be taken as *witnesses* of the corresponding civilization, even if they are impeded and almost nullified by it. And, if in certain primitive periods the spirit of the time is a religious spirit, then its true art is an evasion and a drama, and something of a prophecy; for in such periods all other expressions cannot be poetical, but only symbolic and practical. *Ab Jove principium Musae*—neither language nor poetry originates from religion but only the deities of language and poetry, the symbols and rituals of art, the literary genres, the Muses. But a true time of freedom, in its fleeting course, fashions the language and the art of happiness; and sends back into heaven, with the rest of the gods, the sisters Musae—to hide in the divine Father, which men, in all innocence, have by that time forgotten.

# VI.

# BLOOD

For man's indifferent unity, for the woods' fearful darkness, the religious spirit substitutes organized serfdom, and the gods of the garden. For a silence heavy with every possible word and every conceivable poem, a practical means of communication, consisting of symbols and prayers. For the mysterious fusion of man and woman—the reciprocal slavery of love. For the relationship of resemblance, derivation and unavoidable severance between fathers and sons—the Saturnian deity, the sacrifices on the mountains, and civil war.

But sacrifice of freedom, of poetry and love is not enough to confer certainty and truth upon the gods of the state, born of the ambiguousness of human relations. These idols of identity and separation are one with man's soul, for the soul of man is at once identity and separation. This soul, when free, is both individual and universal spirit; but being every time unable (and desperate) to reach the happy point of free identification, the soul would soon revert to chaos or be reduced to dust, unless it turned its own self, where these relations have their place and where the state resides, into a symbolic object of religious adoration. In other words, state-idolatry is an idolatry of the individual soul, unable to achieve the freedom it requires: it is also the need to find an external, enduring certainty—in human relationship a certainty of life, the persistence of heredity through the generations. Soul, life, permanence in time are therefore a necessary idol and a necessary victim. But what is each man's soul and life? What is each man's continuance through time and children?

"Blood is the life of all flesh; the blood of it is for the life thereof; therefore I said unto the children of Israel: Ye shall eat the blood of no manner of flesh, for the life of all flesh is the blood thereof; whosoever eateth it shall be cut off." * ". . . And I have given it to you upon the altar to make an atonement

* Leviticus, XVII, 14.

for your souls; for it is the blood that maketh an atonement for the soul." *

Blood is sacred, being the very soul; common to all men and every man's own; gushing out entirely from a single wound and eternal through infinite generations. Therefore every god sprung from the need of human relation, every deity of the soul, every symbol of permanence and certitude, holds sacred the blood of man—and blood *alone* can create him. Solemn oaths are sealed with blood; friendship too is a compact of blood. Insults are washed out in blood. Blood engenders mythical dynasties; political outrage, alone, founds tyrannies. Blood raises terror, needless bloodshed is a major sin, a blasphemy. To mention blood is for the Puritans (so attuned to the sacred) the most fearful of curses. Blood is shameful: woman shall be unclean for seven days, and untouchable. Blood is precious: the donors of blood are considered almost heroes for their harmless and easy donation. Blood is a sacrifice which every life requires, it is life itself: woman, this sacred part of man, must shed her blood to know man and to beget man. Blood appears in mysterious dreams. Blood

* Leviticus, XVII, 11.

gives birth to idols: while men were born from the dragon's teeth, the blood of men feeds both gods and dragons.

Every divinity which takes the place of the human soul and life requires therefore the sacrifice of human blood. This blood will have to be *shed*, that is poured forth, expelled from the living body, spilled out of the warm, hidden veins, made extraneous to that of which it was the life, and offered on the altar. Only the shedding of human blood makes real the human deities. Without blood, the sacred wedding would not be true: merely a *marriage*, * instead of holy *matrimony*. The blood-stained sheets are displayed for all to see, and this alone brings forth the matrimonial angels which are to bless the harmony of wedlock. Circumcision in blood introduces the new-born babe to the covenant with that God which it confirms. The Saturnian deities require the bleeding of the sons; the fathers must slay the first born in order not to lose the secret attributes of the divine. And the idol-like states are born only in the outpouring of blood, the blood of their own sons and of the enemies, in the mystery of human sacrifice, in the red act of war, begetter of gods.

---

* That is: *marital* privilege.

Personal deities, humanized beasts, double-faced monsters, idols of the individual self, of the family, of the social group, as well as those gods which attend to certain activities or trades or functions of life, or which preside over love, require the sacrifice of human victims, and these deities spring to life the very moment in which the victim dies. The gods themselves must die to procreate: so that the world might be engendered from pre-existent unity, a god—according to the Hindu tale—had to quarter himself in a Bacchic way, to lacerate and slash and cut himself to pieces. And the insects and butterflies, animals perfectly divine, die when they lay their eggs, or are killed while fecundating the female. Men have to die in order to engender the gods: they have to part with their own selves—not merely with their freedom, but even with their blood, the blood they cherish. Blood flows on every altar of every human god, in every clime and every time. Only a greater capacity for symbolism, as well as the aging and decline of faith, permits the sacrifice of animals' blood instead of man's, or the offer of a supposedly equivalent gift, as a reminder of this precious blood. When Bacchus *omestes*, changed from an Oriental god into a Grecian myth, he allowed the Thebans to offer up a goat

instead of the formerly human victim; and despite
the contrary advice of the people, who knew the
demands of their bull-headed goddess, King Agesi-
laus, according to Plutarch, could sacrifice to the
ferocious Diana a deer instead of a maiden. And
upon the altars of the same goddess, in memory of a
more lethal blood, the youths of Sparta were beaten
with rods. The Peruvians used the blood of children,
drawn from a little wound on the forehead, to make
sweet cakes for the people to eat, in memory of idols,
already archaic, which in their days of power were
made, materially, of human blood. And in Egypt
sacrificial animals were branded by the priest with
a mark representing the true victim—a man on his
knees, with his hands tied behind his back and a
sword about to behead him. But human sacrifice is
completely abolished only with the final fall of the
human idol: for these two amount to exactly the same
thing. When Lycaon is punished by being changed
into a wolf while immolating a child to Jupiter
Lyceus, when Hercules causes Diomedes, king of
Thrace, to be devoured by his own mares, which he
used to feed on the flesh of strangers, it means the
end of the ambiguous, beastlike idols, the freeing of
man from his own monstrous nature, the death of

fauns and centaurs. The substitution of a ram for Isaac is a polemic substitution, directed against idolatry, in confirmation of a God entirely transcendent —requiring a victim which has to be not real, but merely symbolic. Hence the abhorrence of blood, the complete interdiction of shedding blood or of eating it with meat, actions which in themselves are idolatrous: for blood creates the idols and is itself an idol. The animal's blood is not allowed to remain in the meat, or to be shed outside the Tabernacle: and if anyone be guilty of killing an animal elsewhere, "blood shall be imputed unto that man: he hath shed blood, and that man shall be cut off from among his people." * Blood is idol and demon, and generates idols and demons.

As long as the deity and the idol coincide, sacrifice must remain absolutely material: and where the idol is human, the victims must be human too, for every god must die in order to gain life. Substitution of the victim takes place only when the god, ceasing to be an idol, leaves the earth and the body and makes his ascent to heaven and the conscience; for how is it possible to kill a hidden god, a god no one may see nor call by name? Strictly speaking, sacrifice should

* Leviticus, XVII, 4.

be abolished altogether, even in its symbolic form: but, although God is transcendent, he leaves behind some Law, some symbol of the divineness of moral conscience, as an idol of enduring certitude—and to this Law, to this Covenant are due the symbolic sacrifices. Identification of man and God cannot arise without divine and human blood, without the blood of Christ. But this blood too, outside the person of Christ, is still for men a mere symbol, a wine, a religion, and that which ought to be the truest liberty remains even now a practical and ritual liberation.

The Gods must die and bleed in order to exist.

"For where a testament is, there must of necessity be the death of the testator . . . Wherefore neither the first testament was dedicated without blood . . . For when every commandment had been spoken by Moses unto all the people according to the law, he took the blood of calves and of goats . . . and sprinkled both the book and all the people, saying: This is the blood of the covenant which God hath enjoined unto you . . ." *

"It was necessary therefore that the copies of the things in the heavens should be cleansed with these"

* Epistle to the Hebrews, IX, 16–20.

85

(with the animals' blood); "but the heavenly things themselves with better sacrifices than these. For Christ entered not into a holy place made with hands, which is a figure of the true; but into heaven itself . . ." *

"Neither by the blood of goats and calves, but by his own blood, he entered once into the holy place, having obtained eternal redemption." **

Once, says Paul, and forever: the sacrifice of God should be the last of human sacrifices. But the idols live on forever, in the contemporaneity of times, through thousand shapes forever renewed, and men die in adoration upon their altars, or in the forsaken fields beneath a closed sky.

If Christ himself is born of blood, if every man hopes to become immortal, to become a god by way of his own true death; how can the divinity of the state originate without killings, slaughters and war? Banners are sacred only when stained with the blood of citizens, and the greatest national monument is the tomb of an unknown soldier.

For the state-divinity, war is a perfect sacrifice, the victims offered up being the enemies, those who are

---

* Epistle to the Hebrews, IX, 23–24.
** *Ibid.*, 12.

strangers to the god; and also the god himself, his representatives, the members of the state, the warriors. Those among the enemy who have not been killed in battle rightly become slaves—and the slaves are sacrificed on the altars, or spared for servile tasks: victims, always, of the same idol. Conversion is useless, often impossible, seldom offered; proselytes are not required, but strangers to the particular god and to mankind itself, strangers fit to be immolated. Only when a more universal deity stands beside or above the god of the state, is it possible to conciliate opposed interests and differing cults, so that the prisoners are speedily and collectively baptized, as the Spaniards did to the Mexicans, whom they initiated to the kingdom of heaven, before exterminating them *ad majorem Dei gloriam,* to the glory of that other god, who reigned in Madrid over his earthly kingdom. However, baptized or not, converted or not, the spoils of war are always *opimae,* sacred to the goddess of state, host to be sacrificed.

Every war is a duel of gods, a judgment of God, in the double sense of judgment: for God is both the judge and the judged. Only the victorious god is judged to be existing and true: victory is the proof of his birth and of his power, and of his sacred legitimacy. Slaughtering prisoners and defeated enemies is not only legitimate, but imperative in religious war—and it is foolish and pointless to be shocked by the bombing of open cities and the death of infants, in battles fought for the sake of an idol. These prisoners and vanquished, these women and children are not protected by gods, they have no idols of power and life; and thus they do not belong to the world of rites, they are aliens, vanquished people, doomed to be bound in chains, turned into slaves and immolated as victims: *victi* and *victimae*.

Wars follow and mirror the nature of the god for whom they are waged and with whom they merge. The manifold deities of heroic times live in continuous individual contests; feudal deities war on all frontiers, on every level, in every estate. Divinities belonging to large, national and imperial states, wage more extensive wars, national and world-wide. But always the idolatric sense of the state requires war, ceaseless and total, a war which is one with the state and the state's existence, inseparable from the life of the god.

Only the state of liberty is a state of peace: where there is true peace, there is true freedom, for idols cannot live without war; but men live only in peace.

It is peace, because the human person, in its particularity, forms the entire state, and the state, in its particularity, is all person, all mankind. Nothing is extraneous to the state—to the state of liberty—in the true sense of this maxim (which is generally used in reverse): it means that nothing human is alien to man, when man has not assigned limits unto himself, when his freedom allows him to reach at the same time personal individuation and limitless universality. But everything is foreign to the state, when the state is an idol, a limit, and therefore in itself a thing providentially foreign. Everything must become extraneous to the state, for the state can live only at the price of such a mutilation. The divine sentence: "Nothing outside the state," * means, in fact, religiously speaking: nothing shall remain alive of that which is extraneous to the godlike state; everything and everybody shall be victims, so that the state may become a god; there is no life for the state except war. In a free way, the sentence should mean, on the contrary: everything is human, everything is a relationship of human freedom, nothing exists outside human relations, outside the state: therefore, there are no strangers, and hence no vic-

* Mussolini's slogan.

tims; there is no other possible reality for the state but peace.

But for those barren men, who are divorced and severed from sacred aboriginal chaos, there is neither state nor common weal. Nothing is in the state; and therefore peace and war are without meaning: war, for barren reason, is an incomprehensible madness, and peace—a practical and negative ideal, a useless and lifeless absence of war.

The sacrifice of the defeated enemy is a necessity of religious war: hence, the frightfulness of war, which increases in proportion to its sacredness and to the love bestowed upon the national banner. The enemy's blood represents the blood of the idol: the state must bleed in order to live and conquer; to die for one's country is therefore a sacerdotal privilege. War is the business of free men, of citizens, and not of slaves: the warrior class is jealously restricted. Therefore, in times heroic, war is nothing but duels of illustrous champions, contests between military seniors, and the people do not fight, the people only serve under the tents, and carry the burdens, and feed the horses, which are driven by heroes of minor rank. Feudal wars are restricted to the knights, and the peasant troops consist not of fighters but of mili-

tary servants. Combat service, and the blood which
has been shed, are the fount of right, the origin of
citizenship and nobility; hence the political strength
of the English yeomanry, for instance. The various
degrees of power and authority within the state are
marked by the various arms: the *hastati*, the *quirites*,
the lictors, the archers, etc. The nobleman, in the
quiet days of the eighteenth century, did not go out
without carrying his useless sword; and the peasant
of Southern Italy, even today, never forgets his anarchical brigand-axe, even when he does not go to the
woods. For the same reason, officers carry a sword
even in time of peace, and they must surrender this
symbol when taken prisoners. Military uniform is
sacred; it is the vesture of a god. The appearance of a
savage warrior, painted white, mottled and monstrous, is enough to put the enemy to flight, because
it is a divine apparition. The figure of the warrior
must be, as far as possible, an exact image of the idol;
so that it may truly take the idol's place in killing
and in dying. Therefore shields and escutcheons
carry the divine image and describe, in religious
language, the state, its origin and nature. Even modern military uniforms are a reminder of the corresponding national flags and skies and landscapes: in

the grey common mimicry, France is sky-blue, Italy green, Germany black and white. The medieval warrior stands in iron armor, locked in its narrowness as in the limits of the feudal domain, plumed with nobility, towering above his shield like a castle above its walls, and with his visor down, forced to silence and pride. The common people's fighters despise the swords, just as they scorn every state-idol; they glory in ignoble weapons, in pitchforks and scythes, in sporting guns, in knives and stones. When they put Justice or Reason upon the altar they sometimes take for a weapon the guillotine, one of the most rationally and legitimately religious of arms: but as long as they are moved by a sacred and free impulse, they need devise no uniforms, for they themselves are not divided from those who are not fighting. With the rebirth of the monster-gods and of the god-machines, our present-day uniforms acquire again a monstrous and picturesque appearance: the typical beastlike shape of the gas mask is a symptom and a proof of the true aspect of our state-idols.

To die in war is a privilege, an indispensable sacrifice cherished by the god of the state. To kill in war is no offence, it is a merit: it is not criminal bloodshed, but the shedding of sacred blood; it is a task of priests and sacrificers. To be killed in war, as a thousand epigraphs point out, is not to die; it means truly to gain immortality, the very immortality of the state, for one dies for the state, instead of the state, under its banners, with its colors. Everywhere, in every time, poetry and mythology have distinguished this death from every other death, and made it the highest ambition, the most dignified end. Even popular tradition gives to such death a form similar to the death of the gods: an Italian war song sings of a dying officer who asks that his body be divided in seven parts; and, for the heroes most admired, a spontaneous legend takes shape, according to which every one of them was killed by a bullet right in the forehead, even if the circumstances of their death were many and various. Only a complete alteration of the state-deities, and the freedoms which result from such a change, allow the Achilles of the *Odyssey* to lament the death of Achilles in the *Iliad*, or enable Horace to tell the story of his own flight, a flight from death heroic.

*relicta non bene parmula* *

Only those who, at war, shed the enemy's blood and

---

* having indecorously thrown the shield away.

their own are able to partake, really and bodily, in the divinity of the state. Never, therefore, are the serfs allowed to touch weapons; and war is preserved, desired, and considered a necessity by those who identify themselves with their own state-idol, war being the only way to preserve both deity and slavery. Continual, but limited war. Savage warriors and feudal lords live only and solely by a war without interruption, which confirms and consecrates their power, a war which allows to increase both the number of slaves and the weight of their chains. But war is limited by the small numbers of fighting men, and, because of its ritual character, by a thousand usages, declarations and ceremonies. The supreme request of those who are not warriors is to gain permission to join the fight, in order to enter the mystery of the state and partake of the hieratic nature of men and citizens.

The gods fight their battles on the shores of the sea, they drive the chariot and wield the spear. A people of serfs stand aside and look on, silent and patient, resigned victims of the god which shall conquer. The rank and file are witnesses of war, as they are witness to the state, through their indifferent servitude. They well know in their hearts that the gods are a necessary evil; and that these gods are all alike, however dissimilar in colors and emblems, in name and appearance, for all of them consist of a ritual mutilation; of a burden which forces every man to bow down—so that instead of getting lost in the infinite blue of the sky, he is forced to remain content with the earth and rejoice in its crops and green grass. The populace feels the dark terror which gives birth to the gods; it knows only too well the vagueness of its own power, the uncertainty of its own limits; it accepts as unavoidable the religious, hereditary bounds. Bondage upon earth to the gods of the earth, and after death—to the gods of heaven. Freedom seems inconceivable: how can one live a life without ties, and follow a law ever new, a limit equal to infinity? War engenders servitude, the deity's life, and death, the deity's blood. The peasant and serf—no partner, but passive victim—watches the heavy warriors passing through his fields with horses and chariots, and the marauders hard on their heels; and he hides in the woods upon their passage.

The idol-state knows but two fundamental castes: the serfs and the warriors. Both castes are victims, the former sacrificing their bodies to the deity in the hardships and toils of work; the latter—their souls and their blood. They are passive, animal, victims, strange to the idol—or on the contrary, active and sacerdotal, made one with the deity itself. In order not to serve, there is but one way, the way of killing and dying. Therefore the right of fighting is the most coveted right, the only one allowing bodily participation in the divinity of the state. This is why the brave flourish of war stirs up the spirits of youth, pouring some heroism in the citizens' hearts,* as if heavenly bugles were sounding liberty eternal. But the sacerdotal image of war is so true and deeply rooted that, even when all men take part in the fighting, they are still considered not as priests, but as servants of the temple—the sacrificer's crown of oak leaves being reserved for the general, while the former slaves turned citizens and soldiers have to be content with the serf's knapsack and the piglike gas mask of the totemic victim. War is a privilege and sacerdotal distinction—thus even in states which proclaim themselves states "of the people," no discipline is conceivable except one that is dictatorial and tyrannical. It is not merely a matter of technique or competence to obey without question one's superiors: it is also a matter of faith. Everything in an army is religious:

---

* *versent quelque héroisme au coeur des citadins.* (Baudelaire)

the military language, which consists of identical commands and evocatory formulas, sharing the nature of prayer and magic; the shape of the weapons, which results from a perfect symbolism even more than from a consummate technique; the appearance of uniforms and medals; the sacred enclosures where the flag is kept untouchable and hidden until the religious ceremony of battle, when it is displayed upon the altar in the field; the virtue of hierarchy and discipline, fundamentals of the military religion; the consecrated slaughter of the enemy, and the ritual death of the priests-idols-victims.

The warrior once had the task of being a living holocaust and of conquering for his god the due tribute of enemy slaves. The army's task is a similar one, though performed with greater completeness, whenever the army, instead of remaining a part and organ of the state (and having therefore to distinguish itself from the servile victims) grows to be the entire state, in its totality. The warrior then becomes a soldier, the privilege of arms becomes military servitude; and it is discipline which keeps the victim and the priest apart. War no longer requires external aims, nor foes to bring into subjection; for it reaches all its aims even without reasons, and without battles:

it furnishes the state with servants bearing testimony, through their very delusion, to the state's power, and offers victims whose blood inspires the state with a godlike soul.

The structure of the army is a mirror of the social religion. The hero battles all alone; the paladin rides through vales and woods to find his match among the knights. In the aristocratic states there is a class of warrior noblemen, and to join those who bear arms is one of ambition's highest rewards, worth striving for through civil struggles. Peoples without state-religion, such as the Chinese and the Neapolitans, despise the soldier, almost as if he were a murderer. The decay of state-religiosity turns the privilege into profession: auxiliary troops, mercenaries, make their appearance; the vanquished peoples themselves are turned into soldiers, instead of being made slaves. In times of liberty, if armies are raised in defense against an antiquated institution or surviving foreign idols, the entire people are soldiers, while officers and generals are improvised; and the casualties, freely accepted, confirm a community which is not afraid, and has no need of self-worship. Here fighting is no longer only a privilege; it is a moral necessity, a duty—and it does not give the fighter a

98

place among either the masters or the servants. In every other case, heroism is religion, and the army is a church. A ground-swell of freedom, rolling through the centuries, unites with the Jacobins' religion of liberty, and raises from the furrows a people in arms. Through the mere memory of this enthusiasm and of this faith, they sweep on, to the very limits of the world.

Later on, a purely juridical liberalism (the true "religion" of liberty) had to draw the distinction between what is duty and what is right in the bearing of arms for the state's service; and, as the terms of liberalism were entirely functional, it was no longer possible to speak of military privilege, or honor; or of military slavery or sacrifice—but only of military *service*, which is an obligation for all alike, and is accepted by all as a voluntary burden. However, in this juridically unimpeachable form, the army, while belonging to everybody, remained nevertheless what it was before: a church, with its own ritual, its own castes, its sacred emblems and sacred discipline; in short, a state, a god, in contradiction with abstract liberalism, and even more so—with such concrete liberties as could live under the veil of this abstraction. The First World War

hurled to their death those ambiguous citizens'
armies—and many soldiers deemed themselves to
be fighters for freedom who after having over-
come, through war and blood, every social and historical difference and every servitude, were uniting
at last with the entire state in a free community of
people. Others felt their participation to be a truly
ritual one; they slaughtered victims, enjoyed it, and
rightly believed that they alone—the sacrificers—
could form the divine state; and these became, forever, the veteran fighters. Still others died, or resigned themselves to serve. However, the fact that
the entire people is called to arms without becoming
the entire state, and that they must contribute to the
war their bodies and their blood, while taking part
in the state only through a juridical fiction such as a
delegation of powers or plebiscitary approval, is
nothing but a paradox, an evident contradiction.
Universal participation in the ritual of war should
abolish servitude and state-idolatry, and it should
serve therefore as the visible sign of human liberty.
In consequence, wherever state-idolatry, inherited
from the fathers or born anew, was strongest, there
had to be a bolstering up of military discipline,
—that is, a distinction between two different kinds of

fighters: the priests and the servants of the temple. There was established a voluntary militia, a privileged warrior caste, with special arms, and uniforms and colors (black, the sacred color of death) and banners. Wars requiring the people's intervention were avoided as much as possible, and it was attempted to wage limited, heroic wars, with a few chosen forces, while leaving the peasant at his plough, away from the weapons, as in the days of the barbarians. Above all, it was attempted to identify the entire state with the army, and to confer upon the army the characteristics of a church, with an ever growing internal military servitude, and a new flowering of ritual. Military religion here becomes identical with the religion of the state: thus only is it possible to wage universal war without giving up slavery. The goose step is an absolute necessity for a servile and churchlike army—and this step is certainly no more strange than the kneelings and bowings and thousand picturesque ceremonies of countless religious cults, official or private. Its ritual virtue resides, precisely, in its absurdity and uselessness. It is a walking in foreign language, a kind of sacred armed dance—just as prayer amounts to speaking in the language of mystery.

101

Those who believe in the necessity of state-idolatry, and therefore of slavery and war, are compelled—in order to involve their entire people in war while keeping slavery untouched—to transform the entire state into an army, and the army into a church. Should the people be warlike, the state would fall from its divine altars. War must be waged not by a free people in arms, but by a mass of serfs organized into an army. The idols of state and army, of the machine and organization must coincide: so that the gods of the state may live, war must be continuous, not interrupted by the semblance of peace; it must be total, organized and mechanical. The warrior's severance from war must be made manifest, war must become inhuman, out of reach for the single fighting man, the performance of symbolic monsters and of incomprehensible bureaucratic agencies. In short, on the one hand the entire people must be organized into a churchlike army so that slavery may survive, and on the other hand war must be suffered and borne, but not really fought, by a people of slave-soldiers, in order to prevent the privilege of freedom, which belongs to the warrior, from becoming universal and abolishing the worship of the state. It is no easy task to fulfill these two requirements: therefore, on every side, there is little determination to wage war, and, after war has started, to fight it in a thorough and bloody fashion.* The people's wars engender liberty; and liberty makes every war futile. But state-idols live only upon wars; and they need peoples to wage them. And this makes necessary the modern and military organization of the state.

War is a rite, and as such needs no justification. Or rather, war is most efficient and divinity-breeding when it seems absurd and incomprehensible to reason. *Justified* wars, those that are waged in order to protect one's own life or one's own soul, are not religious wars, and therefore have no idolatrous efficiency. Only unjustifiable wars create power and life for the idols of the state. A prayer, to be efficacious, must have little meaning; war, to be useful for the state-divinity, must have no justification. Victims, in whatever religion, need to be perfect: if animals, they should be sound in body; if humans, they should have no faults, or defects, or diseases; the true victim is pure and innocent. Some people are still of the opinion that war is a violent means to solve definite material questions, which, of course,

* Written in 1940.

would be solved even better around a conference table, but which, unfortunately, may be decided quite legitimately by a trial of strength, provided that every other means has proved impracticable. These people believe therefore in the possibility of arbitrating disputes and they deplore the bombing of open cities or the sinking of ships without warning. But they forget that there can be no more reason for war than there is for prayer: that the only reason for war is the lack of reason (for, wherever there is reason, there is no war); that true and efficient wars are only those which have no justification; and that only innocent victims can serve as divine nourishment, and be palatable to the gods.

"Reasonable wars," and peoples' armies, belong to a purely juridical conception of liberty. But true liberty, not the merely institutional freedoms, knows nothing of war, for it has already won all wars, and knows nothing of armies, for it has destroyed them all; and whenever liberty has to fight in order to defend itself against renascent gods and resurgent armies, it means that freedom was not entirely true and not entirely free. Every war waged by liberty is an interior struggle, an enrichment, an increase of peace, a civil war: that civil war which never has a beginning and never shall have an end, just as the chain of birth and death has no beginning and no end. Expressions of the selfsame pharisaism are the conventions for the humanization of war, the protection of the civilian population, and so forth. The milder customs of war derived merely from the waning and decline of the religious sense of war, and from the transformation of certain warlike ventures into purely commercial undertakings, such as colonial wars, the conquest of oilfields, mines, etc.— as well as from the existence of a real religion of humanity and abstract liberty, in opposition to the religion of state. But war cannot be *humanized*, because it is divine. The prisoner must be sacrificed. Civilians, women and children may be spared and forgotten by the warrior, who does not grant them the privilege of dying; but wherever there are no true warriors any more—merely armed and servile masses—there cannot be any privileges nor distinctions. Women and children are part of the mass, and to spare them is a sacrilege.

War weighs down upon the masses, although they take part in it, as a tremendous obscurity, as a phenomenon of nature, indifferent and mysterious. The cold stars of winter glitter in their familiar abodes in the cloudless sky; but from the four corners of heaven there swoop down, like angels or demons, the wings of the bombers. The howl of the city's sirens, in the gray dawn of the roofs, is the voice of war, and its sacred language. A machine is speaking, a machine is fighting, and the man inside is no longer a warrior or really a man: he has merged with the machine and assumed its indifference, its certainty; together with it, he has turned again into a double monster, a beastlike monster of remote antiquity. A new ambiguity is taking shape, a mechanical and sportive association of power and servitude. A thousand new Orions, evil and smiling, are out to hunt through the great forest of heaven. At the roar of their horns the dragons of old awaken, and blood, ready to be shed, throbs violently in every heart, which is filled with ancient terrors and the most ancient hopes.

# VII.

## MASS

More ancient than any memory, more vague than
any hope, more remote than birth itself, there dwells
in every heart an unlimited darkness. Like the
shadow of a body at the rising or setting of the sun,
this darkness narrows or spreads out with the rise or
decline of each person—always, however, persisting.
Behind all luminous actions and thoughts there is
this leisure of the world, this black margin of eternal
passivity, this necessary nothingness, this bottomless
contradiction from which all things originate, measureless and without termination. It is an absolute
with no limits, and therefore with no existence, like
its opposite—finiteness absolute—which, if we may
trust the philosophers, is a self-contradictory concept. But this non-existence is the negative limit of

every living individuation; it is the chaotic condition of every birth; the hollow cave of love. It is
shapeless matter, heavy with all weight, lacking all
quality, and full of every passive potential.

Bakers call "mass" the dough before it is divided
into loaves to become bread in the oven; for metal-
founders "mass" is the melted metal before it is
cast into the mould; for physicists—that which in a
body is neither shape, nor size, nor quality, but indeterminate matter. Mass appears to every individual as a "not me," unavoidable though non-existent,
and which for every physical body is a non-quality,
the negative origin of all qualities, and constitutes,
in the field of human relationship, a non-state, a
formlessness, from which arises by contradiction
every organism of state. It is indeterminate human
material, which is one, and therefore incapable of
relationship, although it holds within itself, within
its non-existence, all possible future relations. The
mass is nothingness, it is sleep and anarchical oneness; it is the negative image of the state. From its
infinite indifference arise men and states, but every
birth, every nation, is a fracture of the mass, a de-
crease of that shadow which constitutes both their
origin and their limit.

Its equally non-existent opposite, anarchical multiplicity, the impossibility of the state, is finiteness absolute, the abstract individual, and old age. History is nothing but the eternal venture of the human mass in its laborious endeavor to determine itself, to resolve itself into state, poetry, liberty, or to abscond into religion, rite, custom; and of the continuous resurgence of the mass from the drying-up of the states and the crystallization of religions. The mass dwells in each of us, hidden in a depth far deeper than conscience and memory, for it is itself the sacred limit of memory and conscience. In the great individual body of a people, mass is pure matter, outside historical conscience and recollection. Mass, in a people, is everything which has no shape, and which strives obscurely to separate, to segregate, and to originate as a person and a state. A mass, therefore, is not the people, not even its lower part, the plebe, nor any social class in particular; but it is the indeterminate crowd, which tries, with the anguish of the mute, to express itself and achieve existence. The characters of Faulkner are a mass—human beings of a still mutable shape, which could, materially, take on monstrous forms; they try in vain to tell themselves apart from their fellows, under the crude light of August which equalizes all things in its harshness; driven by an obscurely common blood, they attempt, in a furious rebellion, to break away from the undifferentiated matter out of which they have been arbitrarily shaped—like sunken bubbles which rise again towards the surface of the sea. In the swarming of the crowd, they cannot really talk and establish human relations, because none of them has any limits, and none of them is yet really born. Their expressions are outcries, killings, prayers— and the atmosphere is one of continual fright, caused by that which is happening and by that which can never happen, and by the incomprehensibility of the continuous attempt.

In every origin there is this formless humanity; and it appears again whenever human intercourse becomes inaccessible, and similar to a mysterious idol perceived by men not as a creation and relationship, but as a destiny. Destiny throws all men together into a common aboriginal equality, and, being indifferent, makes them undifferentiated again.

War, waged by men, but severed from men and incomprehensibly divine, a necessary sacrifice to the divinity of the state, not only disrupts certain definite relations existing between men, but tends to bring men back to that undifferentiation which precedes relationship. A law of death, inhuman like nature, rules everybody's lot; and chance (a chance which men have caused, but which is a mystery to every single man) chooses among them and destroys them. Blood, this liquid shapeless life, covers the earth as a sign of aboriginal community. Physical pain, the suffering of the body, which is an equal burden upon all men, is a daily occurrence, awaited for the morrow. Names are forgotten; a uniform conceals everybody alike in an invisible gray fog. A cloud covers the face of the earth, and in it mankind dissolves, before dying, as if it were a huge indistinct body, wounded and painful, which hides its head and closes its eyes, and nevertheless lives on and spreads like immortal water. Great wars, by themselves, engender the mass: they turn again into a mass which was already determined, and confer a shapeless life to things already crystallized. Every man leaves his house, abandons his own world which was unique to him, merges with all his fellowmen, and after losing everything which made him a person, arrives to that which is indistinguishably common: blood and death.

Great concentrations of people, large cities, also

develop the mass and create it anew. An isolated family, a village, a town of moderate size, do not overtax man's ability to observe and understand: they force him to make a choice, to determine himself by requiring from him a total contribution, not a merely mechanical specialization. But the big city is incomprehensible: one cannot grasp it at a glance, for it lives its own life, the life of a gigantic body through which there runs a blood made of a million unconscious human creatures; and these humans are all alike, living side by side without knowing each other, lost in a boundless resemblance. The city grows at its own margins, like an enormous expanding protoplasm. The suburbs have a tragic appearance, dusty and indeterminate. Vacant lots are covered with fences and wild grass, unexpected walls spring up through the meadows, in the squalid uncertainty of a city which has ceased to be well appointed and of a countryside which has ceased to be bountiful. This shapeless landscape does not display the feeling of things human, or of the things of nature, but only the urge of a life uncertain and equal everywhere, the life of a generical humanity, unable to express itself through the artistry of the buildings or through the orderliness of the fields, and kept out of both, waiting at the door, in patience or in rage. Streets and houses have no definite ending, they only border upon stretches of land no less indefinite: it is the place of a people without history or memories, uprooted from any determination, and with none of the precise colors of a particular hope. The dread of cities hardly arises from the contemporaneity of times upon the paved squares of townships rich in history, trodden by countless dissimilar generations; it does arise from the mystery of boroughs where the silent human crowds are encamped, who have not yet begun to live, and to whom all history is a future.

Where the gods live, men must have an end and hide themselves and find again a contact with their origins. War and city are divine places, where men re-enter the mass. Even work is deified, becoming technique and organization. The factory, grown gigantic, is not understandable to those who live off it, for they are no longer participants but merely tools. Technique, the art of human workmanship and invention, becomes a secret technology, no longer art, but magic. And organization destroys every living organism by imposing upon it its own extraneous divinity. Where there is an organism, there cannot be organization. The latter presupposes shapelessness, and creates shapelessness, to give it a divinely arbitrary order. The works of man, which also constitute a language made of objects, a poetry of things, are not possible any more in a world anonymous, a world without a name, without the gift of speech, unable to express itself, which may labor and slave and pray, but not create. Therefore things become mechanical, they become religious and reproducible expressions, works divine.

Arisen from the mass, and creating the mass, the gods of war, of the city, of the machine, of organization, are nothing but particular aspects, singular expressions and attributes of a greater god, which alone is born of the mass and lives upon the mass—the idol of the state. Mass is infinite repetition, infinite uniformity, infinite impossibility of correlation, absolute impossibility of state—as well as sacred terror before this immense powerlessness, irresistible urge for determination and for unobtainable freedom. Wherever human relations are being established, the mass ends, and man is born, as well as the state. But where the mass persists, with its vague burden and mortal fright, a religion of protection and salvation substitutes for the impossible state some divine symbol, and shapes the mass itself, the non-existent and anguished mass, into an idol which hides it and represents it. The divinity of the mass and that of the state do coincide; the two idols have a single appearance: totality. The dread of absolute and indistinct passiveness, and the dread of liberty, engender, from opposite sides, one single religion: the mass state. As a reality, this concept is contradictory: the state begins where the mass ends; but as a religious expression, the state can be only of the mass. The sacrifices which engender the god and make him true, are, as we have said before, an alienation of the god's very nature; in the idolatry of the state, it is the state itself which has to be sacrificed; that is, for the idol to live, men must turn into mass and come to naught through undifferentiation. Therefore, idol-states need the crowd, and create the crowd, and tend, in conformity with their nature, to suppress every personality and every relationship. Where there is attained, not only juridically, but also in fact, an equality which amounts to shapelessness, and an external justice which amounts to common death, the state is truly divine.

There is no more tongue; the mass, by itself ineffable and silent, truly may find expression only through the state, that is through the religious language of ritual and prayer. Therefore, instead of the spontaneous political and poetical speech, made of innumerable gestures and words, and of relations ever renewed, there appears a sacred language, the language of mass-manifestation, upon the public squares, below the altars of the tribune, in which, as in the classic prayers, the worshipping crowd contents itself with rhythmical replies, such as the *Amen,* the *Ora pro nobis,* the *Kyrie eleison,* and thus feels liberated, as a partaker of the divinity. Wherever the mass is really anonymous, incapable of naming itself and speaking, the sacred language of the state replaces the names, which have lost their meaning, by its own religious and symbolic names: these are numbers, tickets, banners, arm-bands, uniforms, badges, insignia, medals, identification cards, ritual expressions of the fundamental idolized uniformity, and of the idolized uniform organization. Where the spoken word is made impossible by the very nature of the mass, it is useless to speak about the freedom of speech; the law's intervention may at most sanction the non-existence of free speech, and prevent its possible beginning. Those places where there is speech, the high and low Parnassi of political poetry, solemn or vulgar, the parliaments, debating societies and public meetings, the *salons,* and shops and cafés, lose their functions of giving expression to social relations and disappear. Mass-manifestations cannot be expressive: there is no place in them for diversity and thought—only for the oneness of action; not action as freedom, but solely action as passivity, necessity, nature, the weight of undivided numbers: the plebiscite. Poetical language is impossible, and so are art and culture: they must be replaced by religious language, by the ritual of arms, by a certainty capable of repetition. The cities' architecture becomes uniform: to build is no longer to express an ever different personality, but to symbolize an indeterminate power: and therefore, vagueness of feeling must be banished from the symbol, precisely because the symbolized passion—passivity—is indistinct and uncertain. Art grows into monotonous repetition, into a litany, or else it becomes a desperate and impossible groping for freedom, nostalgia or hope. The sense is lost of living relations, for they are replaced by a single relationship, which is symbolic and arbitrary. Cities grow by peripheral progression, like unicellular organisms, and spread through the countryside like a shapeless liquid. Culture, which consists every-

117

where and at all times of a universal and absolute
ability to make distinctions, has no meaning at all, in
the indistinctness of the mass. And thus, instead of
culture, there stands its religious equivalent, a totalitarian, arbitrary will of confusion, which expands,
as matter does, by propagation, and which is valid
not as a value, but as a weight: *propaganda,* the
culture of the masses.

Propaganda is always religious, it is always *Propaganda fides*: to believe in the idol is not to think,
but to adore; it is practical, not poetical expression.
The state does not speak through words, but through
acts of will, like a god; its language is law, and all
law is religious; for it is not the inner norm of a
singular deed, but the external and arbitrary norm
of any possible action. The mass cannot be an organism, which is a moral law, an intimately autonomous
unit; the mass can only be an *organization,* that is an
external, transcendent differentiation, born of a
power extraneous to the mass, which passively persists. The state's existence resides in its external law,
a law efficient and idol-breeding precisely in the
measure in which it is external and arbitrary. Every
autonomy, every act of creation, is, by its very nature, outside this law, inimical to state, a sacrilege.

118

Without the externality of law, the mass would remain immobile, the divine state non-existent. It is necessary therefore that law should be present continually, at every moment of life, (and any distinction between private and public life is meaningless), that law should manifest itself by the evident arbitrariness of its interdictions, commands, and obligatory ceremonies, by the religious solemnity of its ritual, by a spectacular display of uniforms, by the heaviness of the punishments it inflicts.

Since the mass has no limits, its state-equivalent, in its symbolical and hierarchic preciseness, is an idol of unlimited power, to which nothing may be extraneous, and the mystery of which is absolute. To this idol everything must be sacrificed—both freedom and blood. Its necessary rites are total slavery and continuous war. The theory concerning the mass-state finds therefore a most perfect expression in this law, truly sublime in its precision, which commands "to believe, to obey, to fight." * Where the mass is sacred and the state divine, one can neither create nor speak, but only believe and pray. Every autonomous action is sacrilegious and deadly to the idol: obedience alone is required. Furthermore, blood being the

---

* The slogan of Mussolini.

119

soul of the mass, bloody sacrifice is inevitable and providential: only war eternal engenders the gods.

Thus, the mass creates the idol-state; and the idol-state, in its turn, brings mankind back to the primeval condition of a mass. It is the dread of human identity, the impotent need of freedom which forms the religion of the state. Formless man knows nothing outside himself, and therefore cannot know his own self. Infinite repetition of a sacred identical darkness does not amount to multiplicity and life. For the One, even if monotonously repeated, there cannot be Another one: therefore no relation, no activity, no word, no love is possible—only an immense infernal anxiety, and an unconscious striving towards a painful birth. An otherness has to be created: the religious symbol of man's shapeless unity, the godlike state, is appointed to serve as the Other, as the liberating element. But, as the pure passivity of the mass is a non-existence, so also the pure form of the state is no less futile. One does not talk with one's own reflection in the mirror, and the love of the seventeenth-century Narcissus is not love, but death. The image on the water's surface, the godlike state, is really nothing other than the undifferentiated mass—both identical with it and hostile.

The identity between mass and divine state is absolute: both are the selfsame non-existence, viewed as a pure matter or as a pure form. This is the deeper meaning of the prayer, so many times repeated, with such faith, by millions of identical beings moved by a same unconscious inspiration: *Ein Volk, ein Reich, ein Fuehrer.* If the people are a materially indistinct unit, that is, if they are not a people, but a mass, the state is also a unit, formal and arbitrary, a totalitarian idol; and the leader, the one and only leader, shall be truly, materially, exactly the same as the mass, that mass which he does not represent, but symbolizes: for indeed, the symbols of the gods are the gods themselves.

Pure mass is a non-existence; a shapeless death. The pure, divine state is impossible too—a void death. In all eternity, from the one death and the other, freedom and poetry are born; and the mass lives only by the presence of both, and by their continual opposition, which is the continual sacrifice of men to the gods. As long as there are ten righteous men, the city is spared; as long as there remains a single righteous one, the city avoids destruction; only when this one good man is gone, does Sodom perish in confusion. The state-idol can stand only as long as it faces a stranger: a foe which is necessary, which will have to be perpetually expelled, and perpetually discovered again—a providential victim.

Night's darkness dwells in the depth of man: upon the works of man the sun is shining; and when the sun has set, a few stars, or a glimmer in the night, are testimony to the coming morrow. The area of shadow is large or small, according to men and according to the times, and that which is obscure, sacred and shameful is covered by the gods. The dread of human relationship can never be absolute; the word never entirely silenced, the prayer never the only expression; slavery never complete, war never without peace to follow, the state never completely totalitarian. But when the formless extends to a great part of the soul, when sacred terror weighs on the heart, we recognize the power of the state-idol by the sacrifices from which it springs, and by the quality of the holocaust. The god truly reveals himself in the bowels of his dead: divination is, literally, the knowledge of things divine through the bloody language of the victims. The hidden wisdom of sacred things, the true knowledge of religious history, is written in sacrifices and martyrdom. Bowing down to watch the tepid blood which gushes forth from the open bodies, we shall find in it the very face of the god, distinguishable from any other god by the shape of the wounds inflicted. The sacred history of the world is a history of willing servitude, of tortures, punishments and mutilations, of interdictions, expulsions and ritual killings, of slaughter and intolerance, of prisons and exiles. The myriad state-idols are recognized in the myriad victims; each one of these bears upon itself the imprint of the priest, as a witness to mortal faith, describes by the pain it suffers the shape and power of its particular divinity.

# VIII.

## SACRED HISTORY

The myth of the Scriptures is the mysterious tale, the sacred history of man between one death and the other, through the path of religion and liberty. And the venture begins, quite rightly, by an exile, by the loss of Paradise. What is it, however, this sin from which originates every alienation, every enmity, every pain, every death? The myth, taken as a symbol, may have a thousand meanings, all of them equally true: disobedience, pride, lack of faith— and even sexual lust, according to the vulgar interpretation, which is the Milanese and the Dutch one, the Ambrosian and Beverlandian. All the symbolic meanings are equally true: but the letter of the myth is clear, and includes them all in its truth.

The sin of Adam consists in having partaken of a

fruit which gives the knowledge of good and evil. But how could there be sin before the knowledge of good and evil? And how could there be, prior to this knowledge, a prohibition which it was sinful to infringe? Or could it be that the birth of moral conscience is in itself a sin? What is the meaning of the tree, and the serpent with its eternal flattery? What is the sin that engenders death?

A man lived in the garden, and he was free, for he was "a living soul." The word dwelt in him: he alone gave things a name. Moral conscience dwelt in him: he knew that the fruits were good, he knew that his woman was "bone of his bones, and flesh of his flesh," he knew that "a man shall leave his father and his mother, and shall cleave unto his wife, and they shall be one flesh." * Passion was in him, "for deep sleep" was upon him. He was "naked": there was in him an infinite indetermination, but he was "not ashamed," he had no sacred dread of it, because this indeterminateness was at the same time a determination, and nakedness covered itself without need of being hidden. Thus, he was a man, solely and totally man, and lived in the freedom which was the happiness of the garden. Every action was an act of liberty, for it

* Genesis, II, 19.

125

contained in itself its own norm; every work was creative: man was in the garden "to dress it and to keep it," and work was as happy and easy as breathing; every word was a word of poetry, identical with its object and of absolute value: "and whatsoever Adam called every living creature, that was the name thereof." * He was not alone: with him there was a woman, made of his rib, and he lived with her, and with the beasts, and with the trees, and with the lights in the firmament; he was not alone, for he was not separated from them; although an autonomous being, he was at one with all; and because he was not alone, not separated, neither he nor they knew death. His deathlessness was no unlimited extension within a passing time, but eternal contemporaneity of every moment: for this time was not outside himself, nor outside the garden of the world, but concentrated in the eternal liberty of every instant. He was entirely one with the earth of which he had been formed, and the "breath of life" that was breathed into his nostrils may have been nothing but the mist which "went up from the earth, and watered the whole face of the garden." ** Could it be that Adam was the man made

---

* Genesis, II, 6.
** *Ibid.*, 6.

upon the sixth day, in the image and after the likeness of God *—or was he another one? The sacred
book does not explain it; but certainly he was a man,
not God, and his freedom was human, not divine,
like his conscience, like the eternal time and place
of his life. He dwelt in the human land of liberty,
for within him the earth and the spirit—his own
particular nature, and universal value—were indissolubly united. The garden of the world was Adam
himself—and within him there could be no distinction of good and evil, for evil was possible only in
an *outside*, in going out of one's own self, and out of
one's absolute freedom. Adam was entirely man and
the entire man, and in man there is no place for sin.

But the fruit of the tree in the midst of the garden
was the fruit of sin, (which is at one and the same
time knowledge and punishment), for it was the
fruit of divinity. One who eats of this fruit shall be
"as a god"—he shall separate and distinguish himself, and remove himself from the garden and the
world, and look at them from the outside. Thus do
good and evil originate, and "the knowledge of good
and evil"; thus ends the freedom of moral law that is
innate in things, and thus starts the serfdom of the

---

* Genesis, I, 26.

external, of the religious law. The eyes of Adam
saw the world from the inside: they did not need to be
opened in order to see. Once the fruit had been eaten,
his eyes were "opened" upon an outside world, which
is the world of separation. Man becomes a god, in the
effort of self-individuation and of severance from
things, and looks even at himself as at a thing, for—
having made himself a god—he is separated forever
from his own self. But this thing, at which he is look-
ing from the outside, has no shape, for it is at one
with the world, and cannot be really seen from the
outside, no outside having any existence whatsoever.
Therefore this thing is naked—that is sacred and
shameful. The eyes of Adam are opened to behold
something frightful, something which ought to be
covered and hidden, and dismissed. The time of liberty, which was real time, and therefore time eternal,
becomes, when seen from the outside, a material
time flowing into death: and thus the tree is mortal,
and Adam must revert to dust. The interior law of
freedom becomes the external law of sin; confusion
comes in, and separation, and idolatry and sacrifice.
The Lord God, who intervenes and expels Adam, as
also the tempter snake, is nothing but a poetical
impersonation, a hypostasis of man himself: indeed,

expulsion is nothing else than the eating of the fruit of divinity, and temptation is sin itself. Having put his law and poetry and life outside himself, Adam dwells no more in freedom, he is no longer in the garden. His love is no longer love, but amorous tyranny and servitude: "thy desire shall be to thy husband, and he shall rule over thee."* Begetting ceases to be a bliss, and becomes an effort and a pain, torn between power and separation: "in sorrow thou shalt bring forth . . ." Creation turns into fatigue and slavery: "in the sweat of thy face shalt thou eat bread."** The world, instead of true, is symbolic—monsters and idols are born; the serpent becomes a worm, and life a war, ending in death. Perpetuity which would be reached by eating of the tree of life, could not be the eternity of each instant, could not be freedom, but a divine timelessness, which develops to no end—the non-existent time of the gods. Thus, the tree of good and evil is but the external law—separation, idolatry. Therefrom does sacred history begin: man, in order to become a god, drives himself out of his own self, expels, exiles and kills himself; in vain does he strive throughout eter-

* Genesis, III, 16.
** *Ibid.*, 19.

129

nity to reach again his paradise lost, by consecrating victims in his stead, by driving them out, by exiling and killing them, so that he may not die, so that he may become at least a god, if he may not any longer remain a man. His idolatrous death continues through the generations and times, until a god has become man—that is, until again the moral law has taken the place of external law, and freedom the place of tyranny, and heavenly Jerusalem the place of earthly Babylon. Until in man every distinction has been abolished: "There is neither Jew nor Greek, there is neither bond nor free, there is neither male or female; for ye are all one." * If the law is not sin, "by the works of the law shall no flesh be justified . . . , for through the law cometh the knowledge of sin." ** There can be neither freedom nor justice as long as the law resides outside things, in divine estrangement.

But the coming of Christ is also a myth, like the sin of Adam: and in reality fall and redemption are eternal and ever present. Redemption cannot happen once and forever, any more than sin occurred once

---

* Epistle to the Galatians, III, 28.
** Epistle to the Romans, III, 20.

and for all at the beginning of time. A ceaseless fall
and a ceaseless renascence make up history: and when
liberation becomes religion, then liberation is useless. "For if righteousness is through the law, then
Christ is dead in vain," says Paul.* Sin, therefore,
is man's inability to be free and to give a norm unto
himself; it is the search after a law of eternal
certitude, a transmutation of liberty into a religious
symbol, the fear of God, and accordingly—the fear
of self, that self which man has turned into a god. For
this particular god the world becomes transcendent,
and thus incomprehensible and full of fright: everything turns into an idol and requires sacrifice, everything becomes a temple which hides a sacred being.
Original sin, the one and only sin, is separation, the
religion of man. Man becomes god and therefore
victim—and to be god, he must separate from himself, leave the garden, and shed his brother's blood.
He must be a tyrant and a slave, and render inimical
and strange his own work and his own love, and tear
apart body and spirit, and live in anguish, under a
yoke, only to shed his own blood upon the altar.
He must put the word outside the things, and life

* Epistle to the Galatians, II, 21.

outside life; but "the word is nigh thee, in thy mouth and in thy heart."*

Separation, despair, idolatry, are found in all times, and never had a beginning—and freedom, as life itself, is always present. Sacred history puts sin at the beginning of time, for time in its external development is sin itself, and before sin it did not exist. Liberty, the paradise regained, is placed at the end of time. If at the start there is exile, then at the end there is apocalypse, Revelation, a mysterious tale where everyone may find, clearly expressed, his own peculiar story; the second and final narration of Adam's sin, and of the return to the garden, which can only happen through the death of death, through the end of separation, of law, of idolatry, of slavery, and of symbolic substitution. The sin which has to end is man's worship of a thing human, of a beastlike idol, which is an heraldic animal, a monster well adored, a state-religion, war and slavery. It is the serpent, the red dragon, the beast coming up out of the sea, to which the dragon "gave his power, and his throne, and great authority." ** This beast utters great things and blasphemies, in religious language,

---

* Epistle to the Romans, X, 8.
** The Revelation of John, XIII, 2.

and leads people into captivity, and kills men with
the sword. It is the other beast coming up out of the
earth, which deceives them that dwell on the earth
into making and worshipping images, and brings it
about "that as many as should not worship the image
of the beast should be killed";* ". . . and all, the
small and the great, and the rich and the poor, and
the free and the bond, that there be given them a
mark on their right hand, or upon their forehead;
and that no man should be able to buy or to sell,
save he that hath the mark, even the name of the
beast or the number of his name" ( . . . which is
"the number of a man: . . . six hundred and sixty
and six").

It is the great harlot, "that great city, which
reigneth over the kings of the earth" ** and sitteth
upon many waters, of "peoples, and multitudes, and
nations, and tongues," *** and upon the beast,
which is a king, of scarlet color, full of blasphemies;
and which is drunk with the blood of saints and of
prophets, and of all those who have been killed upon
earth; "and upon her forehead was a name written:

---

* Revelation, XIII, 15.
** *Ibid.*, XVII, 18.
*** *Ibid.*, XVII, 15.

Mystery . . ." * Babylon the great shall be destroyed, the city of slaughter and slavery, of mystery and religion. The new paradise, the heavenly Jerusalem, is liberty regained. "And I saw no temple therein: for the Lord God Almighty and the Lamb are the temple of it." ** The city has no mystery, it is of "pure gold, as it were transparent glass. . . . And the city had no need of the sun, neither of the moon to shine in it," ***—for the city itself is light, and there is an end to that separation which needs to be lit from outside. No more enclosures and limits: the gates shall in no wise be shut. No more darkness, or light of the law, for "there shall be no night there; and they need no candle, neither light of sun; for the Lord God giveth them light; and they shall reign for ever and ever," ****—that is, in a time found again, where there is no before and no after, no day and no night, but where every moment is eternal.

That the poetical, and so truthful story (true only in the ever repeated, infinite experience) of Paradise lost, Redemption and Apocalypse, the story of

* Revelation, XVII, 5.
** *Ibid.*, XXI, 22.
*** *Ibid.*, XXI, 23.
**** *Ibid.*, XXII, 5.

134

the rise of human religion, of its liberation and of its ending, has been taken literally and has become a dogma, a law, a religion—is added proof of the tale's profundity and of the truth of its interpretation. For men, incapable of liberty—who cannot stand the terror of the sacred that manifests itself before their open eyes—must turn to mystery, must hide and worship as a dark symbol, the very *revelation*, the shining light of truth.


*La Baule, September—December 1939.*